Intermediate Japanese workbook

Michael L. Kluemper & Lisa Berkson

TUTTLE Publishing

Tokyo │Rutland, Vermont│ Singapore

"Books to Span the East and West"

Tuttle Publishing was founded in 1832 in the small New England town of Rutland, Vermont [USA]. Our core values remain as strong today as they were then—to publish best-in-class books which bring people together one page at a time. In 1948, we established a publishing office in Japan—and Tuttle is now a leader in publishing English-language books about the arts, languages and cultures of Asia. The world has become a much smaller place today and Asia's economic and cultural influence has grown. Yet the need for meaningful dialogue and information about this diverse region has never been greater. Over the past seven decades, Tuttle has published thousands of books on subjects ranging from martial arts and paper crafts to language learning and literature—and our talented authors, illustrators, designers and photographers have won many prestigious awards. We welcome you to explore the wealth of information available on Asia at **www.tuttlepublishing.com**.

Published by Tuttle Publishing, an imprint of Periplus Editions (HK) Ltd.

www.tuttlepublishing.com

Copyright © 2011, 2022 Michael L. Kluemper & Lisa Berkson

Illustrated by Keiko Murakami and Boya Sun

ISBN 978-0-8048-4865-7

Available in This Series:

Beginning Japanese
978-0-8048-4528-1 (paperback)
978-0-8048-4132-0 (hardcover & disc)

Beginning Japanese Workbook
978-0-8048-4558-8

Intermediate Japanese
978-0-8048-4864-0 (paperback)
978-0-8048-5048-3 (hardcover & disc)

Intermediate Japanese Workbook
978-0-8048-4865-7

Distributed by

North America, Latin America & Europe
Tuttle Publishing
364 Innovation Drive
North Clarendon, VT 05759-9436 U.S.A.
Tel: 1 (802) 773-8930
Fax: 1 (802) 773-6993
info@tuttlepublishing.com
www.tuttlepublishing.com

Japan
Tuttle Publishing
Yaekari Building, 3rd Floor 5-4-12 Osaki
Shinagawa-ku Tokyo 141 0032
Tel: (81) 3 5437-0171
Fax: (81) 3 5437-0755
sales@tuttle.co.jp
www.tuttle.co.jp

Asia Pacific
Berkeley Books Pte. Ltd.
3 Kallang Sector #04-01, Singapore 349278
Tel: (65) 6741-2178
Fax: (65) 6741-2179
inquiries@periplus.com.sg
www.tuttlepublishing.com

First edition
26 25 24 23 22   5 4 3 2 1   2205TP

Printed in Singapore

Contents

About *Intermediate Japanese*

Welcome to the second level in a language learning series designed to give you a more natural experience in Japanese language acquisition.

The *Intermediate Japanese* book, workbook, disc, and multimedia materials will help you to gain proficiency in the four aspects of language: speaking, listening, reading, and writing.

The Workbook is designed to help you check your understanding, and to allow you to practice and apply previously-learned and new material.

🔊 Audio files for the Listening Practice sections are available online on the Tuttle website.

The web-based resource for this series, **TimeForJapanese.com**, contains additional learning content and practice tools. Visit it often!

名前： | 月　　日

⬤ Trace the stroke order in the boxes, and then fill in the rest with the *kanji*.

| 漢 | 字 | 子 | 森 | 川 | 州 | 館 | 雪 (kanji practice grid) |

才	一	十	才										
					才						才		

歳	ノ	ト	ヒ	止	屵	屵	岸	岸	岸	歳	歳
歳			歳					歳			

二 Review: Write the following in the most appropriate combination of Japanese characters (*kanji* and *kana*).

1. Let's go. _____

2. This is my friend. _____

3. How old are you? _____

4. Please listen. _____

三 Match the place names by writing the Japanese name in the second column, then write the correct continent in the third column (北 [North] アメリカ,　南 [South] アメリカ, ヨーロッパ, アフリカ, オーストラリア, アジア).

City in English	City in *katakana*	Continent in *katakana*	カタカナ location
5.　Jakarta			アンカレッジ
6.　Mexico City			テヘラン
7.　Anchorage			モスクワ
8.　Paris			リオデジャネイロ
9.　Rio de Janeiro			ワシントン
10. Moscow			メキシコシティ
11. Melbourne			ヨハネスブルク
12. Johannesburg			パリ
12. Sydney			ジャカルタ
13. Tehran			シドニー
14. Washington (DC)			メルボルン
15. Nairobi			ナイロビ

㊃ In the dialogue below, fill in each blank with the correct particle. If no particle is needed, mark X. Some English cues are provided to help you. Then answer the true-false comprehension questions about the dialogue.

和美　：さゆりさん＿＿＿今何歳ですか。
かず み　　　　　　　16.　　　 さい

さゆり：そうですね。私＿＿＿誕生日＿＿＿来週＿＿＿水曜日ですから、まだ十七歳です。
　　　　　　　　　　　　17.　たんじょう び　18.　　　　　19.
　　　　来週＿＿＿木曜日＿＿＿十八歳になります。
　　　　　　 20.　　　　　21.

和美　：じゃ、来年＿＿＿大学＿＿＿行きますか。
かず み　　　　　　　　 22.　　　　 23.

さゆり：はい、北海道大学＿＿＿＊法学部＿＿＿＊入りたいです。父＿＿＿北海道＿＿＿
　　　　　　　ほっかいどう　24.　ほう がく ぶ　25.　はい　　　　 26.　　　　　　 27.
　　　　来ました。おばあさん＿＿＿札幌＿＿＿住んでいます。
　　　　　　　　　　　　　　　　 28.　　　　 29.

＊ 法学部 – department of law
　 入りたい – to want to enter into

Comprehension questions:

30. T　F　Kazumi wants to know how old Sayuri's little sister is.
31. T　F　Sayuri is 17 years old right now.
32. T　F　Sayuri will be going to college in Tokyo.
33. T　F　Sayuri's grandmother lives in Hokkaido.

㊄ You are introducing one of the people pictured below to your teacher. Write out a 紹 介 of 6–8 Japa-
　　　　　　　　　　　　　　　　　　　　　　　　　　　　　　　　　　しょうかい
nese sentences in paragraph form to help you practice. Use the information given, and add some information of your own.

Naomi
age 23
3rd year college student
lives in Tokyo, hobby is music
born in Niigata

Takeshi
age 21
college student
surfs in summer
lives in Yokohama
born in Kyushu

六 Practice the stroke order for each *kanji* below by writing the first stroke in the first box, the first and second strokes in the next box, etc. Fill in remaining boxes with complete *kanji* and the extra rows with previously learned *kanji* you need to practice.

漢												
字												
子												
森												
川												
州												
館												
雪												
才												
歳												

名前：　　　　　　　　　　　　　　　　　　　　　　　　　月　　　　日

① Trace the stroke order in the boxes, and then fill in the rest with the kanji.

自	'	⼍	冂	自	自	自					自
重		自			自				自	自	
	一	⼆	千	千	盲	盲	軍	重	重		
動		重				重				重	
	'	⼆	千	千	盲	軍	軍	重	動	動	
働		動				動					
	⼃	イ	亻	仁	仁	佢	佰	俥	働	働	働
駅	働	働			働				働		
	丨	厂	厂	厍	馬	馬	馬	馬	馬	馬	駅
歩	駅	駅				駅			駅		
	丨	⼘	止	止	牛	歩	歩	歩			
杯		歩							歩		
	一	十	才	木	杧	杧	杯	杯		杯	杯
		杯			杯					杯	

② Review: Write the following in the most appropriate combination of Japanese characters (*kanji* and *kana*).

1. Hakodate is in Hokkaido. _____

2. This is my older sister. She is 18 years old.

_____

3. I go to the store by bus. _____

4. Hiro returns home by car. _____

≡ Read the dialogue below. Write the correct particle on the blank. Particles may be used more than once. Follow the English cues, if provided. Then answer the true-false comprehension questions (in English) about the dialogue.

Setting: Hanako and Akiko are shopping at the 札幌駅 (さっぽろえき), where they meet Erika, an exchange student in Hanako's class at school

花子　　：あ、見て！あの背＿＿高い女＿＿子＿＿私＿＿クラスメイトです。
　　　　　　　　　　　せ　5.　　　　　6.　　7. (topic)　8.
　　　　　エリカちゃん！こっち！

エリカ　：あ、花子さん、こんにちは。お元気ですか。

花子　　：ええ、元気です。今＿＿友達と買い物＿＿しています。こちら＿＿
　　　　　　　　　　　　　　　9.　　　　　　10.　　　　　　　　　　　11.
　　　　　友達＿＿明子さんです。
　　　　　　　12.　あきこ

明子　　：初めまして。明子です。どうぞよろしく。
あきこ　　　　　　　あきこ

エリカ　：初めまして。明子さん＿＿札幌＿＿ですか。
　　　　　　　　　　あきこ　13. (also)　14. (from)

明子　　：いいえ、違います。私は大阪＿＿生まれて、今、東京＿＿住んでいます。
あきこ　　　　ちが　　　　さか　15. (at)　　　　　　16. (in)
　　　　　大学生です。

エリカ　：大学って、どの大学ですか。何＿＿勉強していますか。
　　　　　　　　　　　　　　　　　　17.

明子　　：ええと、昭和女子大学＿＿三年生で、*専門＿＿力学です。
あきこ　　　　しょうわ　　　　18.　　　　　せんもん 19. (topic) りきがく

花子　　：ええ！すごいね！力学って、難しいでしょう。
　　　　　　　　　　　　りきがく　　むずか

明子　　：ええ、難しいです。＿＿、私＿＿戌年ですから、がんばります。
あきこ　　　　　　　　　　20. (but)　21. (topic) いぬ

*専門 – college major
　せんもん

Comprehension questions:

22. T　F　Hanako is from Sapporo.
23. T　F　Akiko lives in Tokyo.
24. T　F　Hanako is a college student.
25. T　F　Akiko's major is not difficult.
26. T　F　Akiko was born in the year of the horse, so she is clever.

四 For each illustration, write a sentence using particle で (by means of ~).

例：父はよく車で札幌から帰ります。

| 27 | 28 | 29 | 30 |

27. _____

28. _____

29. _____

30. _____

五 Practice writing the following *kanji* in the boxes next to them.

自							
重							
動							
働							
駅							
歩							
杯							

名前：　　　　　　　　　　　　　　　　　　　　　　　　　月　　　日

① Trace the stroke order in the boxes, and then fill in the rest with the *kanji*.

読	丶	二	二	言	言	言	訂	計	訪	訪	読
	訪	読			読						
勉	ノ	ク	ク	免	免	免	免	免	勉	勉	
	勉			勉			勉				

② Review: Write the following in the most appropriate combination of Japanese characters (*kanji* and *kana*).

1. My hobby is reading. (use 事) _____

2. I never study at the library. (全然) _____

3. Is it all right to open the window? _____

4. Everyday, I return home by train. _____

③ Draw a simple map of Hokkaido, including neighboring parts of Russia, Honshu, Korea, and China. Label the locations below appropriately (in either カタカナ or 漢字).

Sea of Okhotsk
Hokkaido
Honshu
China
Korea
Sea of Japan
Pacific Ocean
Hakodate
Sapporo
north
south
east
west

四 Rewrite each sentence, adding another action to what exists using the 〜て-form. Next, restate the sentence into English. The first one is done for you.

例： こちらは祖父です。
こちらは僕の祖父で、89歳です。　＝ This is my grandfather, and he is 89.

5. カフェテリアでお昼ごはんを食べました。

_____

6. おじいさんは弟に地理の本を三冊くれました。　（地理 = geography）

_____

7. 誕生日のパーティーは六月三日にします。

_____

8. 一番美味しい天ぷらはあのレストランにありました。

_____

9. 友達からアイヌの昔話を聞きました。

_____

10. 妹は犬にホットドッグをやりました。

_____

五 For each set of prompts below, write a sentence that matches the English and incorporates ALL of the given words. Add particles and other words and verb endings as needed. The first one is done for you.

例： 家　コンピューター　作文　書きます
家で、コンピューターで作文を書きました。
At home on the computer I wrote the essay.

11. 毎晩　友達　家　数学　宿題　します

_____
Every evening at my friend's house, I do my math homework.

12. ピザハット　ピザ二枚　コーラ四杯　注文します

_____
At Pizza Hut we order two pizzas and four colas.

13. 図書館　新聞　よく　読んで　友達　英語　宿題　します
　　としょ　しんぶん

_____

At the library, I often read newspapers and do my English homework with my friend.

14. 体育館　バスケ　する事　趣味　です
　　たいいく

_____

My hobby is playing basketball in the gym.

15. バス　学校　午前　７：３０　行きます

_____

At 7:30 a.m. I go to school by bus.

(六) Practice the stroke order for each *kanji* below by writing the first stroke in the first box, the first and second strokes in the next box, etc. Fill in remaining boxes with complete *kanji* and the extra rows with previously learned *kanji* you need to practice.

読											
勉											
自											
動											
働											
駅											
歩											
杯											

名前：　　　　　　　　　　　　　　　　　　　　　　　　　月　　　　日

一 Trace the stroke order in the boxes, and then fill in the rest with the *kanji*.

王	一	丁	干	王		王					王	
				王						王		
主	`	二	十	宁	主		主		主			主
			主		主				主			
住	ノ	イ	亻	亻	住	住	住			住		住
			住			住		田				
田	丨	冂	冂	田	田			田				
		田										
町	丨	冂	冂	田	田	町	町	町		町		
		町							町			

二 Review: Write the following in the most appropriate combination of Japanese characters (*kanji* and *kana*).

1. I studied English, and then listened to music.

   _____

2. Every night at 5:45 p.m. I walk (return) home.

   _____

3. Kosuke was born in Hiroshima.

   _____

4. The animal I like the most is the tiger.

   _____

三 Write one sentence below each image describing an action taking place. Use the 〜ています form.

5. _____ 6. _____ 7. _____

_____ _____ _____

8. _____ 9. _____ 10. _____

_____ _____ _____

四 Choose a particle that fits each usage. You may use particles more than once. Next, write a sentence that illustrates the use of that particle, in Japanese.

Particle	Usage	Example sentence
11. _____	at/on	_____
12. _____	something that exists	_____
13. _____	signifies a question	_____
14. _____	indicates possession	_____
15. _____	quotation particle	_____
16. _____	follows the direct object	_____
17. _____	also, too	_____
18. _____	but	_____
19. _____	follows the place of action	_____
20. _____	to (w/verbs of motion)	_____
21. _____	from	_____
22. _____	topic marker	_____
23. _____	and	_____
24. _____	until; as far as	_____

五 Write a paragraph introducing your family members. Include age, hometown/home-country, grade or occupation, and birth year (zodiac year). Talk about attributes that seem to agree or disagree with their zodiac animal's personality.

例：家族を紹介します。母の名前はサンディで、四十五才です。先生です。 戌年です。 頭がとても良いです。

_____

_____

_____

_____

_____

_____

六 Practice the stroke order for each *kanji* below by writing the first stroke in the first box, the first and second strokes in the next box, etc. Fill in remaining boxes with complete *kanji* and the extra rows with previously learned *kanji* you need to practice.

王											
住											
町											

名前：　　　　　　　　　　　　　　　　　　　　　　　月　　　　日

一 Trace the stroke order in the boxes, and then fill in the rest with the *kanji*.

教	一	十	土	耂	耂	孝	孝	教	教	教	教	
				教						教		
習	フ	ヲ	习	羽	羽	羽	羽	羽	習	習	習	
入	丶	入										
出	丨	屮	屮	出	出							

二 Review: Write the following in the most appropriate combination of Japanese characters (*kanji* and *kana*).

1. My house is far from school. _____

2. Let's dance tomorrow night. _____

3. Please take out your textbook. _____

4. I am living in Boston. _____

三 Change each sentence into an invitation using the 〜ましょう ending, and then rewrite your sentence in English.

5. 自転車で図書館へ行きます。
　　てん　　　と しょ

　_____

6. お母さんに花を三本あげます。

　_____

7. 船で北海道を旅行します。
   ふね　ほっかいどう　りょこう

   _____

8. カフェテリアでハンバーガー二つとフライドポテトを食べます。

   _____

9. 馬に乗って、海まで行って、帰ります。
   うま　の

   _____

10. 池へ歩いて行きます。
    ある

   _____

11. 電車から降ります。
    お

   _____

12. ニューヨークに住みます。

   _____

13. 自己紹介をします。
    こ しょうかい

   _____

四 Read the story below about Daisuke. Fill in each blank with the Japanese equivalent for each English prompt, conjugating verbs as indicated. When you have filled in all the blanks, answer the comprehension questions at the bottom.

大輔君は札幌で_____。_____が_____から、時々_____
だいすけ　さっぽろ　　14. (was born)　　　15. (ocean)　　16. (near)　　　　　17. (boat)
を_____。月曜日から金曜日まで、お父さんから切符のお金を_____、
　18. (ride)　　　　　　　　　　　　　　　きっぷ　　　　　19. (received from)
お弁当を_____、切符を_____、_____まで_____。
べんとう　20. (take-て form)　きっぷ　21. (buy-て form)　22. (station)　23. (go by walking)
_____は_____。_____も_____。でも、学校まで_____は
24. (plane)　　25. (does not ride)　26. (bicycle)　27. (does not ride)　　　　　　28. (train)
_____。学校の最初(first)の日、_____は_____をします。そして、
29. (rides)　　　さいしょ　　　　30. (students)　31. (self-intro)
_____します。たくさんの_____は近くの_____に_____。
32. (study)　　　　　33. (students)　ちか　34. (town)　35. (are living)
でも、二人か三人の_____は遠い_____に_____、毎日　学校ま
　　　　　36. (students)　とお　37. (town)　38. (are living - て form)
で_____で二時間もかかります。大変ですね。
39. (train)　　　　　　　　　　　　　へん

Comprehension questions:

40. T   F   Daisuke never rides boats.
41. T   F   Daisuke uses his own money to buy train tickets.
42. T   F   Daisuke jogs to the train station.
43. T   F   On the first day of school, all students introduce themselves.
44. T   F   Some students have to travel three hours to get to school.

五 Practice the stroke order for each *kanji* below by writing the first stroke in the first box, the first and second strokes in the next box, etc. Fill in remaining boxes with complete *kanji* and the extra rows with previously learned *kanji* you need to practice.

教														
習														
出														
入														

六 Kanji Review: Below are the new *kanji* from this chapter. Use as many as you can in a short story.

漢 字 子 森 川 州 館 雪 才 歳 自 重 動 働 駅 歩 杯 読 勉 王 主 住 田 町
教 習 入 出

_____

_____

_____

_____

_____

_____

_____

_____

名前：　　　　　　　　　　　　　　　月　　　日

① Match the radical to its meaning and usage. For each radical, write a letter from the meaning column and a *katakana* from the usage column.

	Radical	Meaning	Example usage
1. d., ケ _____	イ	a. crown	ア. 花
2. _____	口	b. power	イ. 海
3. _____	示	c. bow	ウ. 思
4. _____	木	d. person	オ. 国
5. _____	宀	e. grass	カ. 冬
6. _____	力	f. to show	キ. 町
7. _____	冫	g. rice field	ク. 読
8. _____	門	h. ice	ケ. 住
9. _____	言	i. water	コ. 森
10. _____	田	j. enclosure	サ. 聞
11. _____	忄	k. tree	シ. 神
12. _____	弓	l. heart/spirit	ス. 勉
13. _____	艹	m. word	セ. 字
14. _____	氵	n. gate	ソ. 強

② Circle the main radical in each of the *kanji* below.

15. 英	19. 曜	23. 間	27. 暑
16. 寒	20. 話	24. 飲	28. 体
17. 低	21. 池	25. 味	29. 友
18. 頭	22. 売	26. 使	30. 桜

三 Your friend wrote the following introduction. It's too difficult to understand without *kanji*. Write *kanji* above as many of the underlined *hiragana* as you can.

<u>ともだち</u>のゆたかくんは<u>にほん</u>で<u>う</u>まれて、シンガポールで<u>しょうがっこう</u>と<u>ちゅうがっこう</u>に<u>い</u>きました。<u>いまこうこうさんねんせい</u>で、<u>らいねん</u>フランスの<u>だいがく</u>でフランスの<u>ぶんがく</u>をべんきょうするつもりです。ゆたかくんはあたまがよくて、<u>まいにちごじかん</u>もべんきょうします。<u>しゅみ</u>もたくさんあります。ゆたかくんはテニスが<u>じょうず</u>で、<u>ときどきわたし</u>といっしょにテニスをしたりします。<u>うた</u>も<u>す</u>きですから、よくいっしょにカラオケをし<u>に</u><u>い</u>きます。ゆたかくんは<u>ふゆ</u>がいちばん<u>す</u>きな<u>きせつ</u>ですから、スキーとほかの<u>ゆき</u>あそびもとくいです。<u>ふゆ</u><u>やす</u>みにスイスの<u>やま</u>でスノーボードをします。ゆたかくんは<u>しょうらい</u>すごい<u>ひと</u>になると<u>おも</u>います。

四 Draw your favorite *kanji* here and colorfully illustrate it to show its meaning.

名前：　　　　　　　　　　　　　　　　　　　　月　　　日

一　Trace the stroke order in the boxes, and then fill in the rest with the *kanji*.

北	一	十	土	北	北					北
南			北						
	一	十	十	声	声	南	南	南	南
			南					南
西	一	厂	厅	两	西	西		西	
			西				
番	一	二	二	平	平	来	来	番	番	番
			番		番			番

二　Review: Write the following in the most appropriate combination of Japanese characters (*kanji* and *kana*).

1. Please be quiet. _____

2. My sister is a first year college student. _____

3. I played volleyball from 7:30 to 9:30. _____

4. I will introduce my friend Shoichi. _____

☰ Directions: Label the following on the map.

北、南、東、西、本州、九州、四国、北海道、沖縄、札幌、金沢、京都、長崎、
　　　　　　　　　　　　　　　どう　おきなわ　さっぽろ　ざわ　と　さき
広島、那覇　、東京、大阪
　　なは　　　　　　さか

四 In the dialogue below, fill in each blank with the correct words and particle. If no particle is needed, mark X. Some English cues are provided to help you. Then answer the true-false comprehension questions about the dialogue.

あつこ：トム君、どこ＿＿＿＿＿生まれましたか。
　　　　　　　　　　　5. (at)

トム　：ロンドン＿＿＿＿＿生まれて、五＿＿＿＿＿の時から、ワシントンD.C.
　　　　　　　　　　6. (in)　　　　　　　　7. (age/years)
　　　　＿＿＿＿＿住んでいます。父はイギリス人で、母はフランス人です。あつ
　　　　　8. (in)
　　　　こさんは、何年に＿＿＿＿＿か。
　　　　　　　　　　　　9. (were born)

あつこ：私は1990年生まれです。丑年です。ところで、トム君、来週の＿＿＿＿＿＿
　　　　　（うしどし）　　　　　　　　　　　　　　　　　　　　　10. (Tuesday)

　　　　　はひまですか。

トム　　：はい、ひまです。

あつこ：海へ＿＿＿＿＿＿＿か。おだやかなビーチでピクニックを＿＿＿＿＿＿＿。
　　　　　　　11. (won't you go)　　　　　　　　　　　　　　　　　　　　　12. (let's do)

　　　　　おにぎりを＿＿＿＿＿＿＿よ。
　　　　　　　　　　　13. (will bring)

トム　　：海はちょっと…でも、動物園へ行ってみたいです。僕は申年ですから、猿
　　　　　　　　　　　　　　　　（ぶつえん）　　　　　　　　　（ぼく）（さる）　　　　　（さる）

　　　　　は＿＿＿＿＿＿＿好きな動物です。家の北に大きい動物園がありますよ。行
　　　　　　　14. (#1/best)

　　　　　きませんか。

あつこ：猿はちょっと…
　　　　　（さる）

Comprehension questions:

1. T　F　Tom was born in England.
2. T　F　Atsuko was born in the Year of the Horse.
3. T　F　Atsuko wants to have a picnic at the beach.
4. T　F　South of Tom's house there is a zoo.

五 Practice the stroke order for each *kanji* below by writing the first stroke in the first box, the first and second strokes in the next box, etc. Fill in remaining boxes with complete *kanji* and the extra rows with previously learned *kanji* you need to practice.

北												
南												
西												
東												
番												

名前：　　　　　　　　　　　　　　　　　　　　　月　　　日

➊ Trace the stroke order in the boxes, and then fill in the rest with the *kanji*.

右	一	ナ	大	右	右							右
				右			右			右		
左	一	ナ	ナ	ナ	左		左			左		左
				左				左				
乗	一	二	三	千	千	垂	乗	乗	乗		乗	乗
			乗					乗		乗		
降	了	了	阝	阝	阝	陉	陉	陉	降			
		降								降		
首	丶	丷	丷	丷	产	首	首	首	首			
		首					首		首			
道	丶	丷	丷	丷	产	首	首	首	首	道	道	道
		道						道				

➋ Review: Write the following in the most appropriate combination of Japanese characters (*kanji* and *kana*).

1. Please loan me three pieces of paper. _____

2. My Japanese (national language) class is from 9:15 a.m. _____

3. Last week was Father's Day. _____

4. I come to school by electric train. _____

三 Unscramble each set of words to match the statement or question below.

近く　この　銀行　に　あります　か　が。

1. _____

　　Is there a bank (銀行) near here?

右側　あります　に　まっすぐ　行って　銀行　は。

2. _____

　　Go straight ahead and the bank is on the right-hand side.

どこ　あります　は　に　か　郵便局。

3. _____

　　Where is the post office (郵便局)?

渡って　を　次　角　橋　の　左　で　に　曲って下さい。

4. _____

　　Cross the bridge, at the next corner, turn left.

遠い　中学校　は　ですか　ここから。

5. _____

　　Is the junior high school far from here?

公園　中学校　前　の　あります　に　は。

6. _____

　　The park is in front of the middle school.

四 In the dialogue below, Chieko is giving Mark directions. Fill in each blank with particles or words, according to the English cues. Then answer the questions below, in English.

ちえこ：マーク君、放課後、家_____ _____か。
　　　　　　　　　　　　　　7. (to)　　8. (won't you come)

マーク：ええ、行きたいです。家_____どこ_____ありますか。教えて下さい。
　　　　　　　　　　　　　9. (topic)　　10. (location)

ちえこ：学校から21番のバスに_____、東橋と言うバス停で_____
　　　　　　　　　　　　　　11. (ride て-form)　　　　　12. (get off て-form)
　　　下さい。そこから、橋を_____、まっすぐ_____下
　　　　　　　　　　　　　13. (cross)　　　　　14. (walk て-form)
　　　さい。右側に、Lawson's と言うコンビニがあります。そこで、左に_____
　　　　　　　　　　　　　　　　　　　　　　　　　　　　　　15. (turn て-form)
　　　下さい。私の家は左側の三番目の白い建物です。白くて、古いです。

　　_____は旭橋1－2－11です。
　　　16. (address)　　　　　あさひばし

マーク：ええと、学校から、21番のバスに乗って、東橋で降りてから、橋を渡って、
　　　　Lawson'sまで歩く。そして、左に曲がって左側ですね。

ちえこ：すごい！よく分かりました。じゃ、何時に来ますか。

マーク：ええと、分かりません。時計がありません。

Comprehension questions. Circle the best answer:

1. Chieko invited Mark to visit her at _____.
   a) school   b) home   c) a restaurant

2. The first step in Mark's journey is to ride a _____.
   a) horse   b) bus   c) train

3. After that, Mark has to cross a _____.
   a) river   b) parking lot   c) street

4. If he gets hungry on the way, he can stop at a _____.
   a) restaurant   b) grocery store   c) convenience store

5. His destination is on the _____.
   a) right side   b) left side.   c) second floor

6. Mark does not have _____.
   a) money   b) a map   c) a watch

五 て-form Practice: You have an アルバイト at the fruit section of your local スーパー. Your boss has promised you a bonus if you sell more fruit than your co-worker, Tetsuya. Look at these fruits and write down some selling points you might use with your customers. Use the 〜くて form to connect い adjectives but use both い and な adjectives. Some useful vocabulary include:

Useful vocabulary: みずみずしい (juicy), あまい (sweet), やわらかい (soft), じゃくしている (ripe)

例：このバナナは黄色くて、美味しいです。三本で150円です。

バナナ

1. _____

2. _____

もも

3. _____

4. _____

いちご

5. _____

6. _____

りんご

7. _____

8. _____

六 Practice the stroke order for each *kanji* below by writing the first stroke in the first box, the first and second strokes in the next box, etc. Fill in remaining boxes with complete *kanji* and the extra rows with previously learned *kanji* you need to practice.

右									
左									
乗									
降									
首									
道									

名前：　　　　　　　　　　　　　　　　　| 月　　　日

● Trace the stroke order in the boxes, and then fill in the rest with the *kanji*.

枚	一	十	オ	木	朷	朾	枚	枚		枚	
					枚		枚			枚	
的	′	亻	白	白	白	的	的	的		的	
		的					的			的	
新	丶	亠	产	立	立	立	辛	辛	亲	新	新
	新				新		新			新	
古	一	十	古	古	古			古			古
			古		古						
線	く	幺	幺	糸	糸	糸	糸	紅	紀	約	線
	線	線	線		線		線			線	
横	一	十	オ	木	村	杧	栉	样	样	栱	横
	横	横	横		横		横			横	
個	′	亻	伫	们	佪	佪	佪	個	個	個	
		個			個					個	
後	′	′	彳	彳	径	徉	彳	後	後		後	
		後			後			後			

二 Review: Write the following in the most appropriate combination of Japanese characters (*kanji* and *kana*).

1. I speak Spanish. But I don't speak German. _____

2. I travelled from January to June. _____

3. Let's make a cake. _____

4. No, I don't understand. _____

三 Follow the directions below to find the two locations indicated. Clearly mark the route you are to take on the map and label each destination.

家を出て、左に曲って下さい。まっすぐに行って、二番目の交差点の後、左側の二番目の店がハンバーガーショップです。その店でBセット二つとCセット一つを買って木村さんの家まで持って行って下さい。木村さんの家は遠くはないですが、十分ぐらいかかります。

ハンバーガーショップを出て右に曲がって、交差点で右に曲がってまっすぐ行って下さい。二番目の交差点で左に曲がって下さい。そこからまっすぐ行って橋を渡って左側の三番目の家が木村さんの家です。

		郵便局			
北橋					
	花屋		デパート		銀行
新橋					
高校	パン屋	花屋		公園	小学校
		本屋		コンビニ	
		家			
南橋					

四 Using the map above, direct your friend from the high school to your house. Be careful to use the correct particles.

_____

_____

_____

_____

_____

五 Practice each *kanji* below by writing them in vertical columns. Fill in the extra columns with previously learned *kanji* you need to practice.

枚	新	古	線	横	個	後	的					

名前：　　　　　　　　　　　　　　　　　　　　　　　　　　月　　　日

一 Trace the stroke order in the boxes, and then fill in the rest with the *kanji*.

注	丶	冫	氵	沪	汁	汗	注				注
			注							注	
文	丶	亠	ナ	文			文				文
			文			文					
晩	｜	冂	日	日	日′	昈	昈	晄	晚	晚	晩
	晩				晩						晩
宿	丶	宀	宀	宀	宀	宿	宿	宿	宿		
		宿						宿			
少	亅	小	小	少					少		
			少			少					
多	丿	夕	夕	多	多	多					多
		多			多						
調	丶	亠	言	言	言	言	訓	調	調	調	調
	調	調	調			調					
皆	一	上	比	比	比	比	皆	皆	皆		
		皆				皆					皆

階	⁷	³	ß	ß⁻	ßᵗ	ßᵗᴵ	ßᵗᴵ	ßᵗᴵ	阶	阶	階
		階				階					
会	ノ	入	스	合	会	会			会		会	会
		会						会		会		

二 Review: Write the following in the most appropriate combination of Japanese characters (*kanji* and *kana*).

1. I really like the color silver. _____

2. My stomach is empty. _____

3. My legs are not strong. _____

4. How do you say "bridge" in Japanese? _____

三 First, match each counter with its best English counterpart by writing the appropriate letter on the blank. Then, write the appropriate counter for each sentence on the blank in the third column.

1. _____泊   a) floors, stories   レストランはデパートの八_____に
あります。

2. _____階   b) degrees   この旅館に二_____まります。

3. _____枚   c) small round things   家に、犬が四_____とねこが三
_____います。

4. _____匹   d) long cylindrical objects   今年、弟さんは何_____ですか。
    ひき

5. _____本   e) age   今日は暑かったです。99_____でした。

6. _____番目   f) 'th   紙を十_____貸して下さい。
    かみ   か

7. _____個   g) small animals   次の角で右に曲がって、二_____の
信号で左に曲がって下さい。
しんごう

8. _____度   h) nights   傘を何_____持って来ましたか。

9. _____歳   i) flat objects   一人でみかんを七_____食べてしま
いました。美味しかったですよ。

四 You need to buy train tickets to visit your friend in Tokyo. Before you get to the ticket counter, decide to write out all your requests in Japanese. Rewrite the following in Japanese.

1. I want to buy 2 tickets.

_____

2. I want to travel from Osaka to Tokyo.

    _____

3. Is there a transfer?

    _____

4. How much is one ticket?

    _____

5. What time does the train depart (出る)?

    _____

6. Is there a non-smoking car?

    _____

7. (Write another question of your choice here.)

    _____

五 Kazuhisa is trying to make a reservation for a ryokan stay over the phone. To see how well he does, read the dialogue below and fill in each blank according to the English cue. Then answer the true-false comprehension questions about the dialogue.

和久：もしもし、予約をしたいんですが。

旅館の人：はい、分かりました。何_____か。(How many nights will you stay?)

和久：ええと、一泊二日です。来週_____木曜日_____金曜日_____です。
    (particle) (from) (until)
部屋は空いていますか。

旅館の人：ちょっと待って下さい。はい、ございます。何_____様ですか。
    (polite counter for people) (さま)

和久：二人です。和室はありますか。

旅館の人：はい、和室と洋室が_____ございます。和室は二_____に
    (both) (floor/story)
あります。お一人で14,000円です。食事はどうしますか。

和久：そうですね。ご飯は付いていますか。

旅館の人：はい、付いています。晩ご飯は日本食で、朝ご飯は卵やトーストやコーヒー
で、_____です。
    (Western style meal)

和久：いいですね。お風呂は何時から何時まで開いていますか。

旅館の人：お風呂ですか。お風呂は24時間です。_____入ってもよろしいで
    (any time)
すが、男と女は一緒です。

和久：ええ?!

Comprehension questions:

1. T F   Kazuhisa wants to spend two days and one night at the inn.
2. T F   There are rooms available at the inn.
3. T F   The rooms come with breakfast, but no dinner.
4. T F   Kazuhisa expects the bath to be co-ed.

六 Practice the stroke order for each *kanji* below by writing the first stroke in the first box, the first and second strokes in the next box, etc. Fill in remaining boxes with complete *kanji* and the extra rows with previously learned *kanji* you need to practice.

注												
文												
晩												
宿												
少												
多												
調												
皆												
階												
会												

名前：　　　　　　　　　　　　　　　　　　　　　　　　　　　月　　　　日

一 Trace the stroke order in the boxes, and then fill in the rest with the *kanji*.

付	ノ	イ	仁	付	付				付		
肉				付						付	
肉	一	冂	内	内	肉	肉					
				肉			肉				
酒	`	冫	氵	氵	沪	汧	洒	酒	酒		
		酒			酒			酒			

二 Review: Write the following in the most appropriate combination of Japanese characters (*kanji* and *kana*).

1. Turn left at the next corner. _____

2. How much is this notebook? _____

3. One rice bowl with meat (肉丼), one pork cutlet (豚カツ), and two colas, please.
   　　　　　ぎゅうどん　　　　　　　　　　とん

   _____

4. May I drink some water? _____

三 Unscramble each set of words to match the statement or question below.

で　　都旅館　　泊まりたい　　二泊三日　　です　　か
　　みやこりょかん　　と　　　　　　　はく

1. _____
   Do you want to stay at Miyako Ryokan for 2 nights, 3 days?

行って　で　曲がって下さい　三番目　の　右に　角　まっすぐ
　　　　　ま　　　　　　　　　　　　　　　　かど

2. _____

Go straight ahead and at the third corner, turn right please.

に　が　は　私達　予約　あります　8:00
　　　　　　　　よやく

3. _____

We have a reservation at 8:00.

は　を　で　全然　僕　食べません　魚　毎日　レストラン
　　　　　　　　ぼく　　　　　　さかな

4. _____

I don't eat fish every day at home.

を　で　美味しい　注文する　レストラン　とても　ラフテー

5. _____

I will order very delicious raftei at the restaurant.

6. _____

(英語)

四 In the space below, draw a map and label the following locations in Japanese. Use the inside cover of your book as needed.

Taiwan	Naha	Okinawa	Kagoshima
China	South Korea	Pacific Ocean	Kyushuu

五 You want to invite your Japanese friend to a concert and then to a meal out (食事). You have already purchased the two concert tickets, now write out your invitation. Include as much information as necessary and use as many *kanji* as you can. You might include:

A) a greeting
B) the name of the band, the type of music, and why you like them
C) the time and place of the concert
D) directions to the concert hall, which subway stop (地下鉄の駅)
E) a place to eat after the concert (コンサートの後), and what sort of food it offers
F) a meeting place and time
G) a closing

六 Practice the stroke order for each *kanji* below by writing the first stroke in the first box, the first and second strokes in the next box, etc. Fill in remaining boxes with complete *kanji* and the extra rows with previously learned *kanji* you need to practice.

付									
肉									
酒									

七 Kanji Review: When you are introduced to *kanji*, you are introduced to both 音読み and 訓読み. 音読み are written in katakana and 訓読み are written in hiragana. Use the 音読み to order the *kanji* from this chapter in あいうえお order according to the kana chart.

北 南 西 番 東 右 左 乗 降 首 道 枚 的 新 古 線 横 個 注 文 晩 宿 少 多 調 皆 階 会 付 肉 酒

1. _____   9. _____   17. _____   25. _____
2. _____   10. _____   18. _____   26. _____
3. _____   11. _____   19. _____   27. _____
4. _____   12. _____   20. _____   28. _____
5. _____   13. _____   21. _____   29. _____
6. _____   14. _____   22. _____   30. _____
7. _____   15. _____   23. _____   31. _____
8. _____   16. _____   24. _____

名前：　　　　　　　　　　　　　　　　　　　　　　　　　　　月　　　日

一　Trace the stroke order in the boxes, and then fill in the rest with the *kanji*.

| 公 |
| 園 |
| 前 |
| 紙 |
| 絵 |
| 飛 |
| 刀 |

二　Review: Write the following in the most appropriate combination of Japanese characters (kanji and kana).

1. Please show me three photos. _____

2. What is your name? (polite) _____

3. I want to make (do) reservations for two nights._____

4. Please draw (write) a picture. _____

三 Locations and particles: Match each English sentence with the best Japanese sentence. Then fill in the blanks with the most appropriate particle according to the English.

1. ____ The stone is next to the pond.
2. ____ The pond is in front of three trees.
3. ____ The fish is in the (middle of) the pond.
4. ____ The pond is in the west side of the park.
5. ____ Two birds are resting in the (top of) the tree.
6. ____ A cat is sleeping near the tree.

(ア) 池____公園____西____あります。

(イ) 石____池____隣____あります。
　　　　　　　となり

(ウ) 池____木____三本____前____あります。

(エ) ねこ____木____隣____寝ています。
　　　　　　　　となり　　ね

(オ) *鳥____二羽____木____上____休んでいます。
　　　とり　　　わ

(カ) 魚____池____中____います。
　　さかな

*鳥 - bird
　とり

四 Draw a picture of the scene described in Section 3. Add two additional objects of your choice to the scene, and write descriptions of the locations of these new objects below the picture.

1. _____

2. _____

五 Read the dialogue and fill in any missing words/particles according to the English cues. Then answer the comprehension questions about the dialogue.

さとし　　：もしもし、お母さん？

お母さん　：はい、はい、さとし君。何ですか。

さとし　　：僕の＿＿＿＿＿＿＿＿に大事なノートを忘れました。探してくれませんか。
　　　　　　ぼく　　　　room　　　　　　　　　　　　　　　　わす　　　　　　　　　　さが
　　　　　　＿＿＿＿＿＿＿の＿＿＿＿＿＿＿にあると思う。
　　　　　　　　　desk　　　　　　on top of

お母さん　：はい、はい。ちょっと待って。行ってみるわ…。ええと、机の上に何も
　　　　　　　　　　　　　　　　　　　　　　　　　　　　　　つくえ
　　　　　　ありませんよ。

さとし　　：じゃ、＿＿＿＿＿＿＿＿の上には？
　　　　　　　　　　chair

お母さん　：何もないですよ。

さとし　　：じゃ、ベッドの＿＿＿＿＿＿＿＿には？
　　　　　　　　　　　　　　below

お母さん　：ベッドの下？へええ…
　　　　　　さとし君、ノートが*見つかりました。ベッドの下にありました。でも、
　　　　　　ベッドの下に、犬もいました。そのノートはもう、きれいなノートでは
　　　　　　ありません。ばらばらの紙ですよ。

さとし　　：紙！*困った！
　　　　　　　　　こま

* 見つかりました – found
* 困った – to be troubled/stumped
　こま

Answer these questions in English.

1. What happened to Satoshi's notebook?

　　＿＿＿＿＿＿＿＿＿＿＿＿＿＿＿＿＿＿＿＿＿＿＿＿＿＿＿＿＿＿＿

2. Who did Satoshi ask to help him?

　　＿＿＿＿＿＿＿＿＿＿＿＿＿＿＿＿＿＿＿＿＿＿＿＿＿＿＿＿＿＿＿

3. Name two things under the bed.

_____

4. Was Satoshi happy about the outcome? Why or why not?

_____

六 Practice the stroke order for each *kanji* below by writing the first stroke in the first box, the first and second strokes in the next box, etc. Fill in remaining boxes with complete *kanji* and the extra rows with previously learned *kanji* you need to practice.

公											
園											
紙											
絵											
飛											
刀											

名前：　　　　　　　　　　　　月　　日

一 Trace the stroke order in the boxes, and then fill in the rest with the *kanji*.

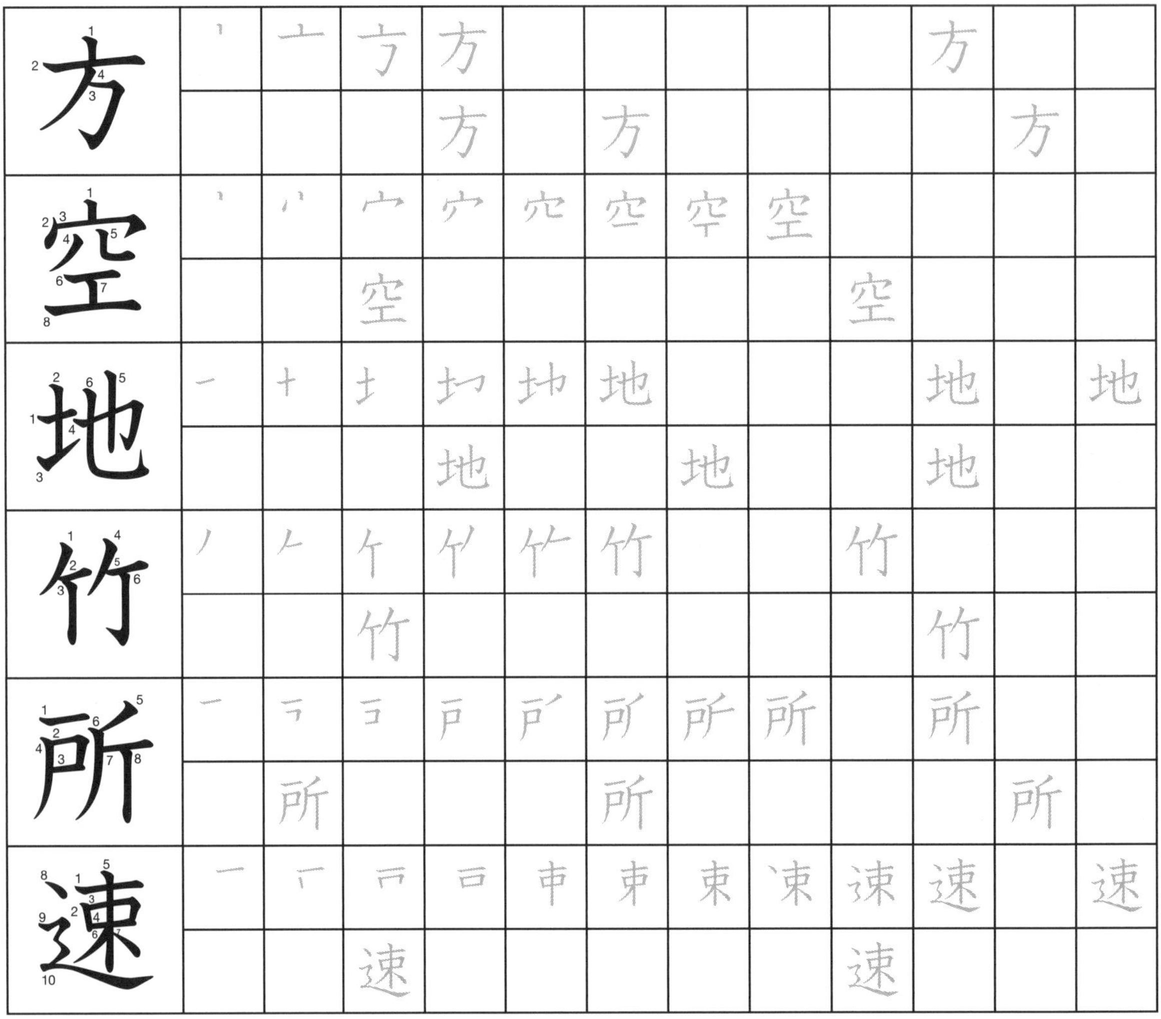

二 Review: Write the following in the most appropriate combination of Japanese characters (*kanji* and *kana*).

1. Please look at this map of Russia. ______________________________
2. That painting is very beautiful. ______________________________
3. Do you have any brighter ones? ______________________________
4. What is the population of Tokyo? ______________________________

三 Use the word bank to write the *katakana* names of each of the 19th century artists below.

1. Degas   _____

2. Monet   _____

3. Picasso   _____

4. Cassatt   _____

5. Gauguin   _____

6. Toulouse Lautrec   _____

7. Van Gogh   _____

8. Whistler   _____

9. Manet   _____

Word Bank
ウィスラー, カサット, マネ, モネ, ドガ, ロートレック, ピカソ, ゴッホ, ゴーギャン

四 Unscramble each set of the following to make a grammatically correct sentence. Use the English translations to help you.

が　より　に　方　の　広島　あります　北　札幌

1. _____
Sapporo is more north than Hiroshima.

の　方　が　西洋的　です　ちょっと　旅館　この

2. _____
This ryokan is a little more Western style.

より　の　方　が　その　近い　デパート　花屋　です

3. _____
The department store is closer than that flower shop.

の　が　もっと　より　あの　ありません　寿司屋　良い

4. _____
There is not a better sushi shop than that one over there.

より　が　の　方　長い　ミズーリ川　です　しなの川

5. _____
The Missouri River is longer than the Shinano River.

五 Combine each pair of sentences into one, using から or だから. Then rewrite the new sentence in English. For the last sentence, write a plausible "result" clause to complete it.

足が痛いです。二階まで歩けません。

1.（日）_____

2.（英）_____

おじいさんは1922年に北海道へ行きました。父は札幌で生まれました。

3.（日）_____

4.（英）_____

先生の話をよく聞きませんでした。宿題は終わりませんでした。

5.（日）_____

6.（英）_____

昨日は雨でした。友達とお城まで遊びに行きませんでした。

7.（日）_____

8.（英）_____

馬が大好きです。カウボーイの映画をよく見ます。

9.（日）_____

10.（英）_____

今日の天気は晴れです。空はとても青いですね。

11.（日）_____

12.（英）_____

この前の冬、雪はあまり降りませんでした。

13.（日）_____

14.（英）_____

六 Practice the stroke order for each *kanji* below by writing the first stroke in the first box, the first and second strokes in the next box, etc. Fill in remaining boxes with complete *kanji* and the extra rows with previously learned *kanji* you need to practice.

方												
空												
地												
竹												
所												
速												

七 Define each radical. Then write as many *kanji* as you can that include that radical. Then construct a sentence using at least three of the *kanji* you have written.

1. 木   [meaning:]

2. 馬   [meaning:]

3. 辶   [meaning:]

4. 糸   [meaning:]

5. 日   [meaning:]

6. 亻（人） [meaning:]

_____

_____

_____

名前：	月　　　　日

➊ Trace the stroke order in the boxes, and then fill in the rest with the *kanji*.

然	ノ	ク	タ	タ	ター	タ	然	然	然	然	然	然
				然		然			然			

➋ Review: Write the following in the most appropriate combination of Japanese characters (*kanji* and *kana*).

1. I never eat meat. _____

2. I do not like talking on the phone very much. _____

3. Red is my favorite color. _____

4. This painting is brighter than that painting. _____

➌ Matching: Read each short description below. Then write the letter for the Japanese artist who best fits that description.

1. _____ 女の人をよく描きました。

2. _____ 富士山が大好きです。海の方へもよく行きます。家は93回変わりました。明るい色が一番いいと思います。

3. _____ 風景を描きました。有名な絵は「東海道五十三次」です。

4. _____ 暗い色が一番いいです。戦争と武士 (warrior) の絵も描きました。

a) 広重 　　　　b) 歌麿 　　　　c) 北斎 　　　　d) 国芳

➍ Use the graphic organizer below to categorize these adverbs. If the adverb can be used with both negative and positive verbs, write it in the center circle. Some adverbs will appear more than once in your graphic organizers.

ちょっと	あまり	少し	いつも	なかなか	とても
よく	けっこう	全然	まあまあ	逆に	たいて

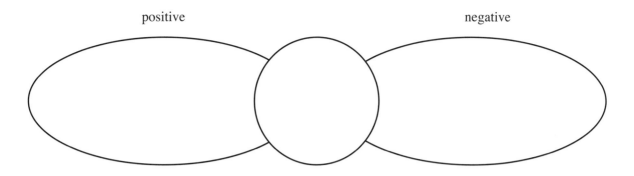

positive   negative

五 Choose five of the words from the previous exercise and write a sentence for each. Be sure to use the correct verb form.

_____

_____

_____

_____

_____

六 Practice the stroke order for each *kanji* below by writing the first stroke in the first box, the first and second strokes in the next box, etc. Fill in remaining boxes with complete *kanji* and the extra rows with previously learned *kanji* you need to practice.

然											

名前：　　　　　　　　　　　　　　　　　　　　　　　　　　月　　　日

① Trace the stroke order in the boxes, and then fill in the rest with the *kanji*.

簡	ノ	ト	ヶ	ヶ	竹	竹	竹	筥	笥	笥	筲	節
単	節	節	節	簡	簡	簡				簡	
弱	丶	丶丶	ヅ	ヅ	屵	屵	当	当	単		単
			単				単		
難	フ	コ	弓	弓	弓	弜	弜	弱	弱	
			弱			弱		
	一	十	廿	艹	芦	苜	芦	莒	莫	莫	莫	莫
難	斳	斳	斳	難	難	難			難	

② Review: Write the following in the most appropriate combination of Japanese characters (*kanji* and *kana*).

1. My hearing is poor (my ears are weak). _____

2. Writing kanji is a little difficult. _____

3. The middle school is farther than my house. _____

4. His older brother is relatively tall. (use けっこう) _____

③ Each comparative statement below is positive. First, restate each in Japanese using より and の方が. Then, use ほど + negative predicate to make a negative comparison.

例：My eyesight is better than my little brother's.
（より）　弟の目より私の目の方がいいです。
（ほど）　弟の目は私の目ほど良くないです。

Today's homework is easier than yesterday's homework. （簡単）

5. （より） _____

6. （ほど） _____

My English teacher is nicer than my French teacher.

7. （より） _____

8. （ほど） _____

My school is larger than my friend's school.

9. （より） _____

10. （ほど） _____

Hiroshige likes blue (color) more than Hokusai.

11. （より） _____

12. （ほど） _____

四 Fill in the boxes with hiragana. Use the dictionary form for verbs.

Down
1. can make
2. can write
3. can see
5. can read
6. can hear
8. capital of Okinawa Prefecture
10. can eat
12. very, considerably
13. afterwards, see you later

Across
3. can show
4. can swim
7. can hear
9. to work
11. can speak
14. can depart, can go outside

五 Practice the stroke order for each *kanji* below by writing the first stroke in the first box, the first and second strokes in the next box, etc. Fill in remaining boxes with complete *kanji* and the extra rows with previously learned *kanji* you need to practice.

簡											
単											
弱											
難											

六 Below you will find *kanji* you know and a couple that you are not familiar with. On each line, write another *kanji* that shares the same radical.

1. 公 _____

2. 園 _____

3. 前 _____

4. 紙 _____

5. 絵 _____

6. 飛 _____

7. 刀 _____

8. 方 _____

9. 空 _____

10. 地 _____

11. 竹 _____

12. 所 _____

13. 遠 _____

14. 然 _____

15. 簡 _____

16. 単 _____

17. 弱 _____

18. 難 _____

19. 早 _____

20. 力 _____

名前：　　　　　　　　　　　　　　　　　　　　　　月　　　日

❶ Trace the stroke order in the boxes, and then fill in the rest with the *kanji*.

早	丨	冂	冃	日	旦	早			早			
				早						早		
力	フ	力			力							
					力							

❷ Review: Write the following in the most appropriate combination of Japanese characters (*kanji* and *kana*).

1. Hurry, let's go outside! ___

2. Because there is a typhoon, the wind is strong. (use 〜から) _____

3. The insect is in the middle of the flower. _____

4. Her older sister never uses a pencil. _____

❸ Adjective and comparisons: Use each adjective pair below to make two comparative sentences. Use より for one, and ほど for the other.

遅い　　　早い
おそ　　　はや

1. _____

2. _____

うるさい　　静か
　　　　　　しず

3. _____

4. _____

明るい　　　　暗い

5. _____

6. _____

多い　　　　　少ない

7. _____

8. _____

㊃ Reread the 会話 section of 3-2. Below, draw the women described there. Then write four phrases in Japanese that describe the picture (e.g., 顔 が白いです).
かお

_____

_____

_____

_____

㊄ Practice the stroke order for each *kanji* below by writing the first stroke in the first box, the first and second strokes in the next box, etc. Fill in remaining boxes with complete *kanji* and the extra rows with previously learned *kanji* you need to practice.

早											
力											

名前：　　　　　　　　　　　　　　　　　　　　　　　　　　　　　月　　　　日

❶ Trace the stroke order in the boxes, and then fill in the rest with the *kanji*.

	一	厂	戸	戸	亘	車	連	連	連		
連				連		連	連	連			

❷ Review: Write the following in the most appropriate combination of Japanese characters (*kanji* and *kana*).

1. Please bring money to school. _____

2. My mother brought my aunt to the concert. _____

3. Which sports are you weak at? _____

4. There are 10 fish in the pond in the park. _____

❸ Rewrite each です/ます statement into INFORMAL (plain) Japanese.

1. 昨日、僕は地下鉄に乗って、東銀座駅まで行きました。
   きのう　　　　　　　　てつ　　　　　　ぎんざ

   _____

2. 西口で友達のジョージに会いました。

   _____

3. ジョージ君はイギリス人で、ロンドンで生まれました。

   _____

4. 僕はジョージ君ほど日本語が上手ではありません。
   ぼく

   _____

5. それから、ジョージ君は僕より勉強が好きで、いつもノートを持っていて、そのノート
   に書いています。

   _____

6. ジョージ君と一緒に歌舞伎座まで歩いて、『ちゅうしんぐら』を見ました。

　　_____

7. ジョージ君は日本のドラマと美術も得意なので、その有名な話も知っています。

　　_____

8. 「日本昔話の中で、どんな話が一番好きですか。」と聞きました。

　　_____

9. 「そうですね。浦島太郎よりもののけ姫の話が面白いと思います。」

　　_____

10. 歌舞伎が終わって、近くの店でおみやげとして*絵葉書を買いました。

　　_____

11. ジョージ君はそのお土産をロンドンまで持って帰って、お母さんにあげます。

　　_____

12. ジョージ君はやさしい人ですね。

　　_____

*絵葉書 – picture post card

四　You are having a party next Saturday, but you need your friends' help. Here is the list you made to remind yourself who is doing what. Rewrite this list in Japanese using the informal speech (plain form). The first one is done for you.

Saturday's Party

1. Reiko will bring yakisoba.
2. Takashi will bring chopsticks.
3. Ayumi will bring a friend and drinks.
4. Yukari will come with Tomoko by bus and bring edamame.
5. Yasuko will bring Masayuki.
6. Hiromi will take Masayuki home by car.
7. I will make a reservation at a karaoke box and buy sushi.
8. (free choice)

1. 礼子さんは焼きそばを持って来る。
   <small>れい</small> <small>や</small>

_____

_____

_____

_____

_____

_____

_____

㊄ Practice the stroke order for each *kanji* below by writing the first stroke in the first box, the first and second strokes in the next box, etc. Fill in remaining boxes with complete *kanji* and the extra rows with previously learned *kanji* you need to practice.

連												

名前：　　　　　　　　　　　　　　　　　　　　　月　　　　日

一 Trace the stroke order in the boxes, and then fill in the rest with the *kanji*.

形	一	二	于	开	形	形	形			形		
			形		形						形	
合	ノ	人	厶	合	合	合				合		
				合		合						

二 Review: Write the following in the most appropriate combination of Japanese characters (*kanji* and *kana*).

1. Go out the door, turn right, and go straight.

   _____

2. What sort of drinks do you like?

   _____

3. The park is wider than the castle.

   _____

4. For three tickets, it will total 15,000 yen. (use 全部で and appropriate counter)

   _____

三 Answer the questions below, replacing the noun with の or 事 in each answer where appropriate. Use the same level of politeness/formality as the question, then rewrite the answer in English. You MAY use the English cues in your answer. The first one is done for you.

例：何を食べる事が好きですか？　　　　　_____納豆を食べるのが好きです。
　　　　　　　　　　　　　　　　　　　　　　　　なっとう

I like eating natto. _____

何に乗る事が好きですか。(riding in an airplane)

1. _____

2. _____

どんな音楽で踊る事が楽しいですか。(rock and roll)

3. _____

4. _____

何の映画を見る事が好きですか。 (scary ones)

5. _____

6. _____

パーティーで何をした方がいいですか。 (playing video games)

7. _____

8. _____

新しい雑誌と昔の本がありますが、どっちが欲しいですか?

9. _____

10. _____

静かな狸ととても元気な狸がいますが、どちらが好きですか。

11. _____

12. _____

近くの旅館かホテルに泊まりたいですが、どちらがいいですか。 (a clean one)

13. _____

14. _____

高い寿司屋とハンバーガーショップを両方知っていますが、どちらで食べますか。
(the closer one)

15. _____

16. _____

四 Sawako is telling her friend Maria a Japanese folk tale about a snow woman, but Maria doesn't understand the informal language. Help Maria to understand the story by writing formal/polite Japanese above all the underlined phrases.

昔々、寒い国での話<u>だ</u>。 茂作と巳之吉の親子 が住んで<u>いた</u>。二人は雪の山に入って動物を*狩るのが<u>上手だった</u>。ある日、とても寒い日に二人は山へ入ったが、吹雪が来たので、山*小屋で一泊することに<u>した</u>。 夜中に吉朗は、山小屋 の外に誰 かが立っているのに気が<u>ついた</u>。外にいた女の人が<u>言った</u>。「あなたを*助けてあげよう。でも、私の事を誰にも言ってはいけないよ。」そう言って、女は山の中に*<u>消えた</u>。

ある雨の日、自分の家の前に一人の女の人が立って<u>いた</u>。女の人の名前は雪子で、吉朗は雨が止むまで雪子を泊めて<u>あげた</u>。いつの日か、二人は*結婚し、子供 も<u>出来た</u>。雪子は料理をするのが上手で、*洗濯するのも得意<u>だった</u>ので、町で有名に<u>なった</u>。

ある雪の日の夜、吉朗は昔の事を思い出して<u>いた</u>。「昔、こんな雪の日に、*珍しい事が<u>あったんだ</u>。」と、吉朗は雪子に<u>話した</u>。「あれは僕がまだ若い時<u>だった</u>。山で雪子のような美しい女に<u>会った</u>。」雪子は、「あなた、話してはいけないと言ったのに。」と言った。そう、雪子は山の中にいた<u>女だった</u>。「どうして*約束を守らなかったの！いつまでも元気でいて下さい。さようなら。」

*狩る – to hunt, 小屋 – hut, 助ける – to help, rescue, 消える – to vanish, 結婚する – to marry, 珍しい – unusual, curious, strange , 約束 – promise

五 Summarize, either in English or by drawing, the folk tale that Sawako was telling Maria above.

六 Practice the stroke order for each *kanji* below by writing the first stroke in the first box, the first and second strokes in the next box, etc. Fill in remaining boxes with complete *kanji* and the extra rows with previously learned *kanji* you need to practice.

形											
合											

名前：　　　　　　　　　　　　　　　　　　　　　　　　　月　　　日

一 Trace the stroke order in the boxes, and then fill in the rest with the *kanji*.

茶	一	十	サ	艹	艾	苂	苯	茶	茶			
				茶				茶		茶	
変	ˋ	亠	广	方	亦	亦	変	変	変			変
				変			変				
品	ˋ	口	口	ロ	ロ	ロ	品	品	品			
				品							品

二 Review: Write the following in the most appropriate combination of Japanese characters (*kanji* and *kana*).

1. We drank tea at the coffee shop. _____

2. The one that is purple is better. _____

3. At the kabuki theatre, we could hear well. (use 聞こえる) _____

4. The population of Edo in 1721 was 1,000,000 people. _____

三 Tomohiro and his friend are at the ticket office at the train station, trying to decide how to travel to Okinawa. Their dialogue is missing some words. Fill in each blank with either one of the choices or according to the English cue. When you finish, circle the correct answers in the English summary and complete the opinion statement, in English.

駅の人　：いらっしゃいませ。

友弘
ともひろ　：沖縄へ旅行する＿＿＿＿＿＿なので、＿＿＿＿＿＿＿＿＿を買いたいです。
おきなわ　りょ　　　　　つもり／はず　　　　　　3 tickets

駅の人　：はい、かしこまりました。何月何日に行きますか。

友弘
ともひろ　：6月10日から6月15日までです。＿＿＿＿＿＿＿＿＿泊まりしたいです。
　　　　　　　　　　　　　　　　　　　　　　　5 nights stay　　　と

駅の人　：飛行機に＿＿＿＿＿＿＿＿＿＿＿＿が出来ますか。それとも、電車に乗る方
　　　　　　　　　　　　　　　riding
　　　　　がいいですか。

友弘 (to 友達)：　どっちにする？

友達：飛行機は電車より速いね。でも、＿＿＿＿＿の方が遠いけど、よく*景色が見え
　　　　　　　　　　　　　　　　　　　　　train　　　　　とお　　　　　　　けしき
　　　る。それに、安いでしょう。

駅の人　：ええ、そうですね。飛行機は速いですが、切符は高いです。
　　　　　　　　　　　　　　　　はや

友弘　：旅館の＿＿＿＿＿も出来ますか。
　　　　　　　りょ　reservation

駅の人　：ええ、出来ますよ。＿＿＿＿＿旅館がよろしいでしょうか。
　　　　　　　　　　　　　　　what kind of

友弘　：僕は古い日本の旅館に泊まりたい。そうしたら、＿＿＿＿＿で、お茶とお菓子
　　　　　　　　　　　　　　　　　　　　　　　　　　Jpn style room　　　　　　か　し
　　　　と美味しい＿＿＿＿＿が出るはずだから。
　　　　　　　　Jpn syle meal

友達　：僕はベッドに寝る＿＿＿＿＿だよ。そして、＿＿＿＿＿に泊まる
　　　　　　　　　　　　つもり／はず　　　　　　　　a cheap place
　　　　＿＿＿＿＿＿だ。
　　　　　つもり／はず

友弘　：じゃあ、一緒に泊まれないね。残念だな。
　　　　　　　　いっしょ　　　　　　ざんねん

　　*景色 - scenery, landscape
　　　けしき

SUMMARY: Circle the correct **bold** answer:

5. Tomohiro and his friend **can** / **cannot** decide on the means of transportation.
6. They **can** / **cannot** decide on the type of lodging.
7. They **are** / **are not** going to travel together.
8. I would like to travel with **Tomohiro** / **his friend** because

---

㊃ The sentences below would be much easier to read if they were written with *kanji* as well as *kana*. Cross out the appropriate *hiragana* and write *kanji* above as many as you can. The maximum number of *kanji* for each sentence is written in parentheses ( ). For extra credit, rewrite each sentence in English.

1. あそこでうごいているものはなに？(3)

2. こうえんまでこのこどもをつれていってください。(5)

3. さんがつみっかはひなまつりです。おんなのこはにんぎょうをだして、あそびます。
　(7)

4. なにどしですか。うまどしうまれです。うまがだいすきです。(6)

5. ちちはかいしゃにまいにちしごとをしにいきます。たいへんですね。(9)

五 Practice the stroke order for each *kanji* below by writing the first stroke in the first box, the first and second strokes in the next box, etc. Fill in remaining boxes with complete *kanji* and the extra rows with previously learned *kanji* you need to practice.

茶												
変												
品												

六 Kanji Review: Use the space below to write as many verbs as you can with the *kanji* you have learned. Use the verb list in the Appendix to help you.

名前：　　　　　　　　　　　　　　　　　　　　　　　｜　月　　　　日

① Trace the stroke order in the boxes, and then fill in the rest with the *kanji*.

葉	一	十	艹	苎	苹	莗	苵	葉	葉	葉	葉	葉
				葉						葉		
忘	`	亠	亡	亡	忘	忘	忘		忘		忘	
				忘					忘			
度	`	亠	广	广	庐	庐	庐	庐	度		度	
				度			度					
非	丿	刂	扌	ヨ	刲	非	非	非				
			非						非			
悲	丿	刂	扌	ヨ	刲	非	非	非	非	悲	悲	悲
		悲							悲			

② Review: Write the following in the most appropriate combination of Japanese characters (*kanji* and *kana*).

1. My friend is expected to go to Osaka. _____

2. Teacher, I'm sorry, I forgot my homework. _____

3. Tomorrow too will probably be very hot, about 35 degrees. _____

4. In college, I intend to study foreign languages. _____

≡ Unscramble the sentences below to match the English version.

侍　住んでいました　ここに　は　有名な
さむらい

1. _____

A famous samurai lived here.

全然　その　分かりません　言葉　は　難しくて
ことば

2. _____

Those words are too difficult, I don't understand at all.

宿題を　忙しかった　出すの　を　忘れた　ので
しゅくだい　いそが

3. _____

Because I was busy, I forgot to turn in my homework.

よく　場所　ので　見える　明るい　は　この
ばしょ

4. _____

Because this place is bright, I can see well.

下　その　の　にある　です　椅子　の
いす

5. _____

It is the one under that chair.

四 Rewrite the sentences below in Japanese using either それで or ので to combine them into one sentence.

1. That picture is beautiful. I want to buy it.

_____

2. The kabuki play "Chushingura" is sad. I don't want to see it.

_____

3. I know the folktale of Urashima Taro. I intend to draw those pictures.

_____

4. Tomorrow is Tom's birthday. I will bring him an awesome present.

_____

五 Refer to the designated 会話 section for this chapter to answer these questions, in English.

1. (2041) What does the kamishibai man do after he tells a story?

_____

_____

2. (2042) List three things that Ben says he can do, and one he says he cannot, in response to Ichikawa's question.

_____

_____

3. (2043) According to Ichikawa's nephew, what are kabuki's lucky colors?

_____

_____

4. (2044) Write down the title of the kabuki play Kiara and her friends are about to see. Also list three of the characters.

_____

_____

六 Practice the stroke order for each *kanji* below by writing the first stroke in the first box, the first and second strokes in the next box, etc. Fill in remaining boxes with complete *kanji* and the extra rows with previously learned *kanji* you need to practice.

葉											
忘											
度											
非											
悲											

名前：　　　　　　　　　　　　　　　　　　　　　　　月　　　　日

➊ Review: Write the following in the most appropriate combination of Japanese characters (*kanji* and *kana*).

1. Can you bring your older brother, too? _____

2. Tokyo Tower (タワー) is tall and red. (use 〜くて) _____

3. Please introduce yourself. _____

4. The convenience store (コンビニ) is behind the post office. _____

➋ Create a sentence using either つもり or はず for each image. Include one of the time words in the box below in each sentence.

例：明日、12時に寝るつもりです。or 明日、妹は早く寝るはずです。

1. _____   2. _____   3. _____

4. _____   5. _____   6. _____
_____   _____   _____

7. _____   8. _____   9. _____
_____   _____   _____

Time Words

明日	明後日	来月	来週	先週	昨日
夏休み	2010年	来年	九月	火曜日	1:45

三 Reviewing comparison structures: Use the map on the inside cover of your book to make statements comparing islands and regions (地方) in Japan. Each sentence should use the cue provided.

1. (use 〜の方が　〜より近い)

   _____

2. (use 〜の方が　〜より遠い)

   _____

3. (use 〜ほど　遠くない)

   _____

4. (use 事が出来る)

   _____

5. (use それで)

   _____

6. (use 〜ので)

   _____

7. (free choice sentence)

   _____

四 Write the meaning of each radical and then write as many examples that include that radical as you can. Use the *kanji* list in the appendix as needed.

Radical	Meaning of radical	Example kanji
心 (忄)	_____	_____
辶	_____	_____
艹	_____	_____
人 (亻)	_____	_____
力	_____	_____
山	_____	_____
木	_____	_____
言	_____	_____
門	_____	_____
車	_____	_____
川	_____	_____
食	_____	_____
宀	_____	_____
夕	_____	_____
子	_____	_____
口	_____	_____

名前： | 月　　　日

➊ Trace the stroke order in the boxes, and then fill in the rest with the *kanji*.

洗	丶	氵	氵	汁	汼	洗	洗	洗			
			洗						洗		
散	一	十	艹	芊	苩	苩	昔	背	背	散	散
			散				散				
浴	丶	氵	氵	氵	浴	浴	浴	浴			
			浴						浴		
湯	丶	氵	氵	沪	沪	沪	湯	湯	湯	湯	湯
			湯				湯				
氷	丿	刂	刂	氺	氷						
			氷				氷				
泳	丶	氵	氵	氵	泳	泳	泳				
			泳						泳		

➋ Review: Write the following in the most appropriate combination of Japanese characters (*kanji* and *kana*).

1. This ukiyoe of Hiroshige's is bigger than that one.

_____

2. Tomorrow morning, let's depart at 6:45 a.m. (use 出発する)
   しゅっぱつ

_____

3. One hamburger and two cups of cola, all together are 1,200 yen. (use 全部で)

_____

4. Let's go with my big brother on a walk.

_____

三 Fill in the missing sections of the chart below.

Dictionary form	verb stem + 方	Example sentence	英語
洗う		兄の服の洗い方は ちょっと珍しいです。	My older brother's way of washing the clothes is a little unusual.
	書き方		The way that student writes kanji is interesting.
		友達の話し方は面白い です。	
		あの犬の飲み方はちょっと 変です。	That dog's way of drinking is very strange.
踊る			That woman's way of dancing is wonderful.
	泳ぎ方		That boy's way of swimming is skillful.
		お箸の使い方が下手です。	
飛ぶ			That bird's way of flying is very beautiful.

四 Use the English cues below to fill in each blank.

1. 治虫君は_____に生まれました。
   15 January 2001

2. 僕はたいてい_____に晩ご飯を食べます。
   5:23 p.m.

3. 妹は_____に生まれました。
   11 July 2009

4. 日本語のクラスは毎日_____にあります。
   9:05 a.m.

5. 学校は_____に始まります。
   14 August

6. _____まで勉強しました。
   11:59 p.m.

五 Developing presentation skills: You have been asked to give a presentation about a story you have recently read, or a movie or television program (テレビの番組) you've seen. Write a short paragraph to help you with your oral presentation. Include an introduction, body, and closing. For example, if you have recently read "Romeo and Juliet," you might write:

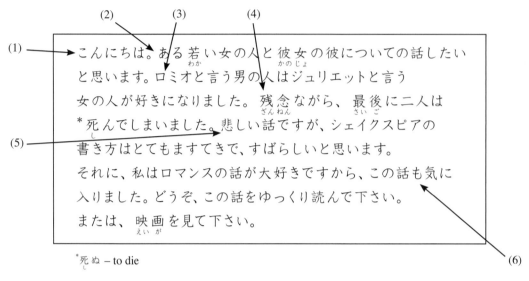

(1) こんにちは。ある若い女の人と彼女の彼についての話したいと思います。ロミオと言う男の人はジュリエットと言う女の人が好きになりました。残念ながら、最後に二人は*死んでしまいました。悲しい話ですが、シェイクスピアの書き方はとてもますてきで、すばらしいと思います。それに、私はロマンスの話が大好きですから、この話も気に入りました。どうぞ、この話をゆっくり読んで下さい。または、映画を見て下さい。

*死ぬ – to die

(1)	greeting	(4)	body, point 2
(2)	introduction	(5)	opinion summary
(3)	body, point 1	(6)	closing

_____

_____

_____

_____

_____

_____

_____

_____

六 Practice the stroke order for each *kanji* below by writing the first stroke in the first box, the first and second strokes in the next box, etc. Fill in remaining boxes with complete *kanji* and the extra rows with previously learned *kanji* you need to practice.

洗											
散											
浴											
湯											
氷											
泳											
忘											
度											
悲											
変											
連											

名前：　　　　　　　　　　　　　　　　　　　｜　月　　　　日

❶ Trace the stroke order in the boxes, and then fill in the rest with the *kanji*.

女	く	夕	女								
			女						女		
男	丨	冂	冂	甲	田	罗	男		男		
			男				男				
温	丶	冫	氵	沪	沪	沪	沪	汨	汨	温	温
			温					温			
泉	'	丨	冂	白	白	臫	泉	泉	泉		
		泉					泉				
若	一	十	艹	艹	芋	芋	若	若			
			若						若		
冷	丶	冫	ソ	冷	冷	冷	冷		冷		
			冷					冷			

❷ Review: Write the following in the most appropriate combination of Japanese characters (*kanji* and *kana*).

1. Is it all right if I bring my friend (informal)? (use 連れて来る)

   _____

2. Writing Japanese is more difficult than speaking. (use 〜事、より)

   _____

3. Please allow me to introduce my friend, Juliet. (紹介する)
   しょうかい

_____

4. There are four girls and three boys in my family.

_____

☰ Choose the best adjective from the Word Bank below for each scenario. Write it on the blank.

1. _____ = a warm cup of coffee

2. _____ = a hot day

3. _____ = a cold bowl of ice cream

4. _____ = a dark room

5. _____ = a bright T-shirt

6. _____ = a complicated problem

7. _____ = a kind person

8. _____ = a sad movie

9. _____ = a lukewarm hot tub

10. _____ = an embarrassing moment

Word Bank

ぬるい	暑い	恥ずかしい	悲しい	暗い
明るい	複雑	やさしい	長い	近い
遠い	変	短い	暖かい	寒い
きれい	汚い	美しい	冷たい	

四 Below is a list of rules for your local bowling alley. Restate them in Japanese for your friend Fumiko, who will be visiting from Hakone. Some of the rules might not be what she is used to at bowling alleys in Japan.

1. You must not wear tennis shoes.

_____

2. You may not wear short skirts.

_____

3. You may not chew gum. (ガムをかむ)

_____

4. It is all right to wash your hands.

    _____

5. It is all right to drink warm drinks.

    _____

6. You may not use a cold (to the touch) bowling ball.

    _____

7. It is all right to make mistakes. (間違う)
        ま ちが

    _____

8. It is all right to wear dark socks.

    _____

9. It is not all right to wear earrings.

    _____

10. You may bowl until 12 a.m.

    _____

11. Free choice

    _____

12. Free choice

    _____

五 You have been introduced to almost 250 *kanji* at this point. Use your favorite graphic organizer to cre-
    atively group and categorize the *kanji* in the Kanji appendix in your textbook. For instance, one group
    could be related to water; one group could be things your friends like to do; and another could be *kanji*
    that are more difficult for you to remember.

（六）Practice the stroke order for each *kanji* below by writing the first stroke in the first box, the first and second strokes in the next box, etc. Fill in remaining boxes with complete *kanji* and the extra rows with previously learned *kanji* you need to practice.

女												
男												
温												
泉												
若												
冷												
洗												
散												
忘												
度												
悲												
泳												

名前： | 月　　　日

一 Trace the stroke order in the boxes, and then fill in the rest with the *kanji*.

近	´	厂	ㄏ	斤	斤	近	近				
			近					近			
遠	一	十	土	士	吉	吉	声	克	克	袁	袁	遠
	遠			遠				遠			
暖	l	冂	冃	日	日´	日	旷	旷	暚	暚	暖
	暖			暖				暖			
比	一	上	比	比			比				
				比				比			
忙	´	㇒	忄	忙	忙	忙		忙			
			忙						忙		

二 Review: Write the following in the most appropriate combination of Japanese characters (*kanji* and *kana*).

1. Go outside and turn left at the first corner.

   _____

2. Tomo is always hungry.

   _____

3. The cat is sleeping below (under) the bed.

   _____

4. Because I did not do my homework, the teacher was sad.

   _____

≡ Your friend started writing a story, but wants you to rewrite it in Japanese. Finish the story in English, then rewrite it in Japanese below.

Long long ago, an old man saw a mouse. "I intend to give the mouse a cookie," he said. The man placed the cookie near the mouse and watched. The mouse didn't want to eat the cookie, but he was hungry. Therefore, the mouse ate the cookie. The cookie was big, brown, soft, and very delicious. The mouse was eating the cookie when he thought "I'm becoming thirsty. May I drink a glass of milk?" he asked the old man.

The old man said "I'm sorry. I wanted to give you some milk also, but I forgot. _____

_____

_____

_____

mouse – 鼠 (ねずみ)	crisp – サクサク
set (to)/place (to) – 置く (お)	soft – 柔らかい (やわ)

_____

_____

_____

_____

_____

_____

_____

_____

四 Make each simple statement below longer and more interesting by adding a modifying clause such as 〜している人 to each sentence. Add details as necessary. Follow the example:

Simple statement	**Statement with modifying clause**
例：大輔君(だいすけ)は生徒(と)です。 →	あそこで勉強している人は大輔君(だいすけ)です。

1. 充子(あつこ)さんは温泉に入っています。

_____

2. トム君は自転車に乗って、学校へ来ます。

_____

3. 友弘君は歌舞伎を見ています。
   ひろ　　　かぶき

_____

4. 私は先生と話していますから、敬語を使います。
                          けい

_____

5. 光子さんはその公園で散歩をしています。
   みつこ

_____

6. マイク君は 牛 乳 が大好きです。毎日飲んでいます。
          ぎゅうにゅう

_____

五 Practice the stroke order for each *kanji* below by writing the first stroke in the first box, the first and second strokes in the next box, etc. Fill in remaining boxes with complete *kanji* and the extra rows with previously learned *kanji* you need to practice.

近												
遠												
暖												
比												
忙												

名前：　　　　　　　　　　　　　　　　　　　　　｜　月　　　日

➊ Trace the stroke order in the boxes, and then fill in the rest with the *kanji*.

浜	丶	冫	氵	汀	汀	汀	泸	泣	浜		
			浜						浜		

➋ Review: Write the following in the most appropriate combination of Japanese characters (*kanji* and *kana*).

1. I cannot draw pictures at all. (全然)

   _____

2. That woman over there is fairly tall. (けっこう)

   _____

3. I normally/usually watch television in the evening.

   _____

4. My little brother can swim well. (〜げる)

   _____

➌ Rewrite the following in Japanese. Pay attention to the tense and whether the statement uses the first person (〜たいです) or the third person (〜たがっている) forms.

   例:　This evening, I want to take my friend to the dance. →
   　　今夜、私は　友達がダンスに連れて行きたいです。

1. Tomoko wants to wash her red dress.

   _____

2. Jun wanted to take a shower.

   _____

3. I did not want to turn at that corner.

   _____

4. My little brother wants to ride a large boat.

_____

5. My mother wanted to write a book, but now she is making a movie.

_____

6. I want to study math in college.

_____

四 In the dialogue below, fill in each blank with the correct word or phrase according to the English cue. Then answer the comprehension questions about the dialogue.

横浜の駅で：
よこはま

出札係： いらっしゃいませ。
しゅっさつがかり

友子さん：奈良へ行きたいんですが、_____の電車は何時ですか。
　　　　　なら　　　　　　　　　　　　　　next

出札係： はい、奈良ですね。10時21分に*急行があります。それから、*特急が
しゅっさつがかり　　　なら　　　　　　　きゅうこう　　　　　　　　　　とっきゅう
　　　　　11時5分にあります。_____ですか。
　　　　　　　　　　　　　　　　how many people (polite)

友子さん：二人です。_____はいくらですか。
　　　　　　　　　　　ticket

出札係： 1_____、2,226円です。
しゅっさつがかり　counter-flat things

友子さん：それから、民宿に_____ですが、駅に近いのを教えて下さい。
　　　　　　　みんしゅく　want to stay at

出札係： はい、かしこまりました。民宿の_____も出来ます。ええ
しゅっさつがかり　　　　　　　　　　　　　　　　reservation
　　　　　と、駅に近いのは、民宿中田がございます。一_____と
　　　　　　　　　　　　　　　　　　　　　　　　　　　floor/story
　　　　　二_____があって、大きいお風呂もあって、朝食付きです。
　　　　　　　floor/story　　　　　　　　　　ふろ　　　　　　ちょうしょく

友子さん：いいですね。_____、いくらですか。
　　　　　　　　　　　3day/2night stay

出札係： そうですね。_____は二_____で、4,452円で、部
しゅっさつがかり　　　　ticket　　　　　　counter-flat things
　　　　　屋はお一人様、2,500円、全部で_____円になります。
　　　　　　　　　　　　　　　　　　　　　fill in total　　　へ

友子さん：はい、それでは、20,000円からお願いします。
　　　　　　　　　　　　　　　　　ねが

* 出札係 – ticket agent, 急行 – express train, 特急 – super-express train
　しゅっさつがかり　　　　　きゅうこう　　　　　とっきゅう

Comprehension questions:

1. T F   Tomoko wants to travel to Kyoto.
2. T F   The ticket agent can only sell train tickets.
3. T F   Tomoko is travelling by herself.
4. T F   Tomoko wants to spend three days at her destination.
5. How much change did Tomoko receive? _____

五 Try to match each 擬声語・擬態語 with the most appropriate situation. Fill in each blank with a *katakana* letter.

1. _____ a messy room   ア）とんとん
2. _____ an overworked stressed worker   イ）ぽたぽた
3. _____ a policeman knocks on the door ウ）グーグー
4. _____ water trickling down   エ）いらいら
5. _____ a sleeping grandfather   オ）めちゃくちゃ

六 Practice the stroke order for each *kanji* below by writing the first stroke in the first box, the first and second strokes in the next box, etc. Fill in remaining boxes with complete *kanji* and the extra rows with previously learned *kanji* you need to practice.

浜													
近													
遠													
暖													
比													
忙													
男													
温													
泉													
若													
冷													

名前：　　　　　　　　　　　　　　　　　　　　　　　月　　　日

⬤ Trace the stroke order in the boxes, and then fill in the rest with the *kanji*.

止	丨	ト	止	止			止			
			止					止		
危	ノ	ク	ク	广	乡	危	危			
		危					危			

⬤ Review: Write the following in the most appropriate combination of Japanese characters (*kanji* and *kana*).

1. This train is faster than that train. (〜より)

   _____

2. This problem is not as simple as that problem. (〜ほど + neg.)

   _____

3. What sort of animal is that? (何の)

   _____

4. Hironori was born in Yokohama but now lives in San Francisco.

   _____

⬤ Fill in each blank box with the correct conjugation of the verb. The last two are free choice.

Dict./英語	plain past	plain neg	plain neg past	potential (える、られる)
出発する/to depart しゅっぱつ				
			始めなかった はじ	
	たべなかった			
		動かない		

Dict./英語	plain past	plain neg	plain neg past	potential (える、られる)
動かす/to move (something)				
	踊った おど			
				会える
		合わせない		
	忘れた			
出掛ける かけ				
			借りなかった か	
求める/to request もと				
(free choice)				
(free choice)				

四 Review the verbs for Chapters 1-5 in the Verb Appendix in the back of the book. These verbs are listed on the following page as well. Decide how to best categorize them so that you can remember them more easily, then label each box below as one of your categories. As you write verbs in the organizer, cross them off the list. Examples of categories are "things I hate to do," "everyday actions," or "actions that are good (or bad) for me." You may choose to use a different graphic organizer on a separate piece of paper.

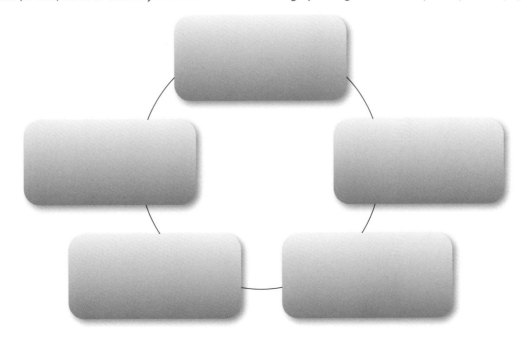

歩く	頂戴(する) ちょうだい	混ぜる ま	出発する しゅっぱつ	合わせる	洗う
歩いて行く	習う	引く ひ	始まる はじ	御座います ご ざ	乾く かわ
歩いて来る	空く	釣る つ	着く	忘れる	浴びる あ
歩いて帰る	教える	注文する	動く	出掛ける で か	亡くなる な
運転(を)する うんてん	似る に	予約する よやく	動かす	致す いた	
乗る	曲がる ま	泊まる と	踊る おど	借りる か	
働く	渡る わた	飛ぶ と	出来る	払う はら	
勤める つと	降りる	過ぎる す	合う	求める もと	

五 Look at the image below. Write four sentences describing four different actions you see in the image. Use the plain past or the plain past negative tense of the verb. Then write four more sentences using the potential form of the same verbs.

(plain past/plain past negative)

1. _____

_____

2. _____

_____

3. _____

_____

4. _____

_____

(Potential)

5. _____

   _____

6. _____

   _____

7. _____

   _____

8. _____

   _____

六 Practice the stroke order for each *kanji* below by writing the first stroke in the first box, the first and second strokes in the next box, etc. Fill in remaining boxes with complete *kanji* and the extra rows with previously learned *kanji* you need to practice.

止											
危											
浜											
近											
忘											
忙											

七 In the space below, write pairs of *kanji* that share radicals. Example: 泳 and 浜.

名前：　　　　　　　　　　　　　　　　　　月　　　日

➊ Trace the stroke order in the boxes, and then fill in the rest with the *kanji*.

夕	ノ	ク	タ		タ	タ					
				タ						夕	
内	丨	冂	内	内		内				内	
				内					内		
朝	一	十	古	古	吉	吉	直	卓	朝	朝	朝	朝
				朝					朝		
昼	フ	コ	尸	尺	尺	尽	居	昼	昼		
			昼					昼			
夜	丶	亠	广	疒	疒	夜	夜	夜			
				夜						夜	
正	一	丁	下	正	正			正			
				正						正	

➋ 復習 Review: Write the following expressions using *kanji* and *kana*.

1. I ate a lot for lunch, so now I want to sleep. (ので)

_____

2. Because there was a small insect on top of the plate, I did not want to eat anything. (ので、何も)

_____

3. His manner of speaking is correct. (～方)

_____

4. Our school's baseball team is the best. (一番～)

_____

三 Fill in the blanks with the equivalent Japanese word or phrase, according to the cue. The last line is for you to add your own ending to the story of Eriko and Mark's day.

えり子さんは家の_____にいて、白いシャツを_____。でも、四時ごろ、
　　　　　　　　　 inside 　　　　　　　　　　　　 wore/was wearing

_____に_____。鳥の声は_____ _____。雨が_____始めました。
 outside 　　went out/exited 　　こえ 　　not at all 　　cannot hear 　　　　fall/precipitate　はじ

えり子さんの白いシャツは_____。そして、_____。えり子さんの_____の
　　　　　　　　　　　　　 became brown 　　　　　　　 became wet 　　　　　　 younger brother

靴_____ _____。四時半ごろに、外は_____。それで、お天気は_____
くつ also 　　became wet 　　はん　　　 became warmer 　　　　　　　　 became clear

になりました。えり子さんと_____のマークは外で絵を描いて、遊びました。
　　　　　　　　　 younger brother 　　　　　　　　　　　　　　　か　　　　あそ

(free choice)_____。

四 Write the English equivalent under each *kanji* (a - e). Then write the letter (a – e) of the time of day that best matches each activity.

(a) 朝　　　　　(b) 昼　　　　　(c) 夜　　　　　(d) 夕　　　　　(e) 晩

_____　　　_____　　　_____　　　_____　　　_____

1. _____ パーティへ行く

2. _____ カフェテリアでハンバーガーを食べる

3. _____ 友達と電話で話す

4. _____ 寝る
　　　　　ね

5. _____ 音楽を聞く

6. _____ 宿題をする
　　　　　しゅくだい

7. _____ 映画を見る
　　　　　えいが

8. _____ テニスをする

五 Practice the stroke order for each *kanji* below by writing the first stroke in the first box, the first and second strokes in the next box, etc. Fill in remaining boxes with complete *kanji* and the extra rows with previously learned *kanji* you need to practice.

夕												
内												
朝												
昼												
夜												
正												
洗												
散												
忘												
習												
度												
悲												
泳												

名前：　　　　　　　　　　　　　　　　　　　　　　　月　　　日

❶ Trace the stroke order in the boxes, and then fill in the rest with the *kanji*.

様	一	十	才	才	术	栏	栏	栏	栏	样	样
	様	様		様						様	様
第	ノ	ト	上	⺮	竹	竹	竺	笫	笫	第	第
		第				第				第	
鬼	ノ	ィ	白	白	由	由	尹	鬼	鬼	鬼	
	鬼					鬼					

❷ 復習 Review: Write the following expressions using *kanji* and *kana*.

1. At New Year's, because friends come to our house, we clean well. (から)

   _____

   _____

2. I can make reservations over (by means of) the telephone. (事が出来る)

   _____

   _____

3. In Akita, we give the demons rice crackers and sake.

   _____

   _____

4. Every year, the fish in the pond become fewer.

   _____

   _____

≡ Respond to each question according to the prompt. Use the prompts in parentheses in your answers.

1. いつ日本に来ましたか。 (We have just come to Japan.)

_____

2. 何時まで勉強しましたか。 (I have just finished studying.)

_____

3. 日本語のクラスにどんな生徒がいますか。 (In the class, there are only good students.)

_____

4. 良和君は、たいていどんなレストランへ行きますか。(He has little money so he only goes to ramen shops.)
よしかず

_____

5. 今日、家で何をしていましたか。 (It's my mom's birthday so I only helped mom today.)

_____

6. 家でお兄さんは何をしますか。 (eats pizza and sleeps)

_____

7. 土曜日にはどの町へよく行っていますか。(I only go to Akita City on Saturdays.)

_____

8. 来週の天気はどうでしょうか。(It is supposed to only rain.)

_____

9. カファテリアで何を食べますか。(I only eat bento in the cafeteria.)

_____

10. 朝、どんな飲み物を飲みましたか。(I only drink coffee in the mornings.)

_____

四 In the space below, transform a *kanji* from Chapter Six into an animate character. It can be a person, animal, or even an anime character. Be creative!

五 Write the correct furigana reading above each of these *kanji*. Then write four sentences using as many of these *kanji* as you can.

図書館	皆	付ける	多い	連れる	朝
読む	社会	公園	働く	忘れる	昼
住む	一番	弱い	動く	悲しい	正しい

(と under 図書館)

_____

_____

_____

六 Use English prompts (cause) to write cause-and-effect sentences using ので.

例：stomachache お腹が痛いので、学校へ行きたくないです。
（なか いた）

1. lost homework

   _____

2. received New Year's money

   _____

3. afraid of the dark

   _____

4. (free choice)

   _____

七 Practice the stroke order for each *kanji* below by writing the first stroke in the first box, the first and second strokes in the next box, etc. Fill in remaining boxes with complete *kanji* and the extra rows with previously learned *kanji* you need to practice.

様											
第											

者
鬼
正
夜
昼
朝
内
夕
遠
近
忘

名前：　　　　　　　　　　　　　　　　　　　　　　月　　　　日

➊ Trace the stroke order in the boxes, and then fill in the rest with the *kanji*.

怖	㇒	㇒	忄	忄	忙	忙	怖	怖			
			怖							怖	
以	㇊	丨	以	以	以			以		以	
			以								

➋ Review: Write the following in the most appropriate combination of Japanese characters (*kanji* and *kana*).

1. I like morning more than evening. (use より)

   _____

2. Kyoko watched the movie and became more afraid. (use 〜て、〜くなる)

   _____

3. Toshihiko is less skilled at tennis than basketball. (use 〜ほど)

   _____

4. This weekend, Mai intends to go shopping in Shibuya. (use つもり)

   _____

➌ Dina and Jacques are both living in Okinawa. Read Dina's email to Jacques, then number the following sections of the letter: 1 – opening/greeting; 2 – small talk ; 3 – body of letter; 4 – closing. Finally, answer the comprehension questions below.

ジャック君へ、

元気？私は毎日忙しいけど、元気だよ。先週の土曜日は楽しかったね。ゴーヤチャンプルーはけっこう美味しかった。今度の土曜日、友達にコンサートの切符を二枚貰って、沖縄の伝統的な演奏のコンサートへ行くつもり。一緒に行かない？20歳以下の人は入ってはいけないけど、ジャック君はもう21歳になったから、心配はないと思う。お正月の特別なのコンサートで、昼から晩までずっと音楽ばかりを聞くのよ。いいでしょう？

行けるかどうか教えて下さい。待っています。

ディナより

Comprehension questions:

1. After what event did Dina write this letter? _____

2. What is she inviting Jacques to do together? _____

3. How long will the event last? _____

4. Are there any age restrictions for the event? If so, what are the restrictions?

    _____

5. What level of formality is this letter? _____

6. Describe the relationship between Dina and Jacques. _____

四 The following is a list of rules posted at the event that Dina and Jacques might attend. Put each rule into English.

1. お酒を飲まないで下さい。

    _____

2. タバコを吸わないで下さい。

    _____

3. 靴をはいて、シャツを着て下さい。

    _____

4. ガラスのものを持って入らないで下さい。

    _____

5. 切符を持っていない人は入ってはいけません。

    _____

6. 20歳以下の人は入ってはいけません。

    _____

五 それでは、それじゃ: for each cue, write a corresponding response, in 日本語、that begins with それでは or それじゃ. Then re-write your response in English. The first sentence is done for you.

例：一緒に行く事が出来ます。それでは、行きましょう。
    I can go with you. So, let's go.

1. 妹さんを連れて来てもいいです。

    _____

2. お腹がペコペコです。
　　　なか

_____

3. 明日の試験の勉強をするつもりです。
　　あした　　しけん

_____

4. うるさい音楽を聞くのが好きです。

_____

六 Practice the stroke order for each *kanji* below by writing the first stroke in the first box, the first and second strokes in the next box, etc. Fill in remaining boxes with complete *kanji* and the extra rows with previously learned *kanji* you need to practice.

怖												
以												
鬼												
第												
様												
正												
夜												
昼												
朝												

名前：   月   日

⊖ Trace the stroke order in the boxes, and then fill in the rest with the *kanji*.

配	一	厂	冂	冘	西	酉	酉	酉ˉ	配ˉ	配		
			配							配		

⊜ Review: Write the following in the most appropriate combination of Japanese characters (*kanji* and *kana*).

1. Don't worry. (〜ないで下さい)

   _____

2. Take out 5 sheets of paper. (枚)

   _____

3. That restaurant has only (just) fish. (ばかり)

   _____

4. That red demon is not as scary as this black demon. (〜ほど〜ない)

   _____

⊜ Choose the best 擬声語 or 擬音語 to complete each sentence below.

ドキドキ	ケロケロ	いらいら	びしょびしょ	にゃーにゃー
パクパク	わいわい	ほかほか	ばらばら	

1. 蛙(frog)の_____鳴く声を聞いた。

2. あらっ！見て！彼がいるよ。_____している。

3. 大雨で、_____になってしまった。

4. 猫が_____とないているから、水をやって下さい。

5. 昨日の数学の宿題は難しかった。_____した。

四 You just received the following invitation. You need to write a note to your friend asking him/her to join you at the event. Use the lines below. Your note might include:

1) opening/greeting
2) weather small talk
3) the time, date, place, and cost of the event
4) a reason for your friend to join you
5) closing

招待状
しょうたいじょう

大晦日を首里城で
しゅりじょう

エイサー踊り　　　沖縄伝統的音楽の演奏
　　おど　　　　　おきなわでんとう　　　えんそう
お節料理　　　　　甘酒
せちりょうり　　　　あま
カラオケ　　　　　羽根突き
　　　　　　　　　はねつ

料金：無料
りょう　むりょう
場所：那覇市の首里城
ばしょ　なは
日時：12月31日午後10時から

_____

_____

_____

_____

_____

_____

_____

五 Practice the stroke order for each *kanji* below by writing the first stroke in the first box, the first and second strokes in the next box, etc. Fill in remaining boxes with complete *kanji* and the extra row with a previously learned *kanji* you need to practice.

配												
鬼												
怖												
以												
若												
冷												
洗												
危												
散												
忘												
枚												
古												
頭												

名前：		月　　　日

⚊ Trace the stroke order in the boxes, and then fill in the rest with the *kanji*.

知	ノ	⽷	⽷	午	矢	知	知	知			
				知						知	

⚋ Review: Write the following in the most appropriate combination of Japanese characters (*kanji* and *kana*).

1. Please close your mouth. _____

2. Do you know that girl over there? _____

3. Ben can sing and dance. (事が出来る) _____

4. Turn right, then walk to (as far as) the third signal(信号).
   しんごう

   _____

⚌ Unscramble the sentences below to match the English version.

そうじ　よく　する　前　お正月　を　に　の
　　　　　　　　　　　しょうがつ

1. _____
   Before New Year's, we clean well.

車　電車　帰る　人々　飛行機　多くの　と　で　が　と
　　　　　　　　　　　ひこうき

2. _____
   Many people return home by car, train, and plane.

お土産　持って帰る　時々　を
みやげ

3. _____
   Sometimes they bring home souvenirs.

としこしそば　家　12時　皆　夜　食べる　一緒　を　に　に　の　で
　　　　　　　　　　　　　　　　　　いっしょ

4. _____
   At our house at midnight, we all eat toshikoshi soba together.

西洋　お正月　面白い　日本　かもしれません　の　の　より　は
よう　　　　　おもしろ

5. _____
   Japanese New Year's might be more interesting than Western New Year's.

④ Kazuhito has invited his friend Jacob to join his family for New Year's. It will be Jacob's first New Year's in Japan, and he has some concerns. Help write each of his questions in Japanese. Suggested grammar patterns are in parentheses.

1. Is it all right to use a fork? （〜てもいいですか。）

   _____

2. Will there be more than 12 people there? （以上）

   _____

3. Will the room become noisy? （〜くなる）

   _____

4. If I watch TV, will I understand? （〜たら）

   _____

5. Have you ever had a foreign guest （お客さん）　before? （〜した事がある）

   _____

6. If I come, then may I bring another guest? （〜たら）

   _____

7. If I eat tofu, I might get a stomachache (my stomach might become painful). （〜かもしれません）

   _____

8. Is it all right to speak English only? （ばかり）

   _____

⑤ Now, take on the role of Kazuhito, Jacob's friend. Below, thoughtfully answer each of Jacob's concerns in Japanese, based upon your best understanding about what would be appropriate in Japan. The first one is done for you.

例：いいえ、フォークを使ってはいけません。日本ですから、お箸を使って下さい。

1. _____
2. _____
3. _____
4. _____
5. _____
6. _____
7. _____

(六) Practice the stroke order for each *kanji* below by writing the first stroke in the first box, the first and second strokes in the next box, etc. Fill in remaining boxes with complete *kanji* and the extra rows with previously learned *kanji* you need to practice.

知											
怖											
洗											
泉											
朝											
冷											
夜											
様											
忘											
昼											
開											
多											
配											

名前：　　　　　　　　　　　　　　　　　　月　　　日

① Trace the stroke order in the boxes, and then fill in the rest with the *kanji*.

治	`	ニ	ミ	氵	汁	治	治	治			
			治							治	
代	ノ	イ	仁	代	代			代			
			代					代			
疲	`	亠	广	广	疒	疒	疒	疓	疲		
			疲						疲		

② Review: Write the following in the most appropriate combination of Japanese characters (*kanji* and *kana*).

1.　There was a volcano here before, but now it is gone. (なくなる)

   _____

2.　I may be travelling to Hiroshima in June. (かもしれません)

   _____

3.　My big sister has read more than half of that book. (以上)

   _____

4.　After lunch, the weather gradually got warmer.

   _____

③ Read the list below. Decide which of these you MAY do (〜てもいいです), which you MAY NOT do (〜てはいけません or 〜てはだめです。), and which you MUST do (〜しなければなりません) at a coffee shop. Then rewrite each statement in Japanese.

例：walk inside the bus　→　バスの中で歩いてはいけません。

1.　pay the bill　　　_____

2. drink a hot drink _____

3. eat with chopsticks _____

4. listen to music _____

5. sit down _____

6. smoke tobacco (〜を吸う) _____

7. talk loudly (big voice) _____

8. go there with a friend _____

㊃ Think of a phrase that can logically complete each sentence. Write your phrase in the blank. Then rewrite the completed sentence in English.

1. _____ば、寝られません。

2. 英語：_____

3. 手を洗えば、_____。

4. 英語：_____

5. _____ば、高い時計が買えます。

6. 英語_____

7. 急に車を止めれば、_____。

8. 英語　：_____

9. _____ば、イタリアレストランで美味しいピザが食べられる。

10. 英語：_____

11. アルバイトがあれば、_____。

12. 英語：_____

㊄ Draw a picture of you and a friend in a 喫茶店 that you have visited or that you know about. On the following page, write two sentences in Japanese that might appear in your conversation with your friend. Use the pattern 〜した事がある in both of your sentences.

1. _____

2. _____

六 Practice the stroke order for each *kanji* below by writing the first stroke in the first box, the first and second strokes in the next box, etc. Fill in remaining boxes with complete *kanji* and the extra rows with previously learned *kanji* you need to practice.

治												
代												
疲												
知												
配												
鬼												
内												
昼												
夜												

名前：　　　　　　　　　　　　　　　　　　　　　　　　月　　　日

一 Trace the stroke order in the boxes, and then fill in the rest with the *kanji*.

漫	`	ミ	ミ	シ	沪	沪	沪	沪	沪	沪	温
	浸	漫					漫			漫	
画	一	厂	戸	而	而	面	画	画			
		画					画				
由	l	口	日	由	由			由			
		由						由			

二 Review: Write the following in the most appropriate combination of Japanese characters (*kanji* and *kana*).

1. Morning is the best time to (take a) walk. (一番良い)

　　_____

2. Jun studied only kanji. (ばかり)

　　_____

3. She is tired, so she must rest. (ので、〜なければなりません)

　　_____

4. Bill is from Alabama. His speech (way of speaking) is a little calm. (話し方)

　　_____

三 For each season, create four sentences that go with that season about something you:

A. want (〜が欲しい)　　　　　　　　　　C. want to do (〜がしたい)
B. don't want (〜は欲しくない)　　　　　D. don't want to do (〜はしたくない)

例：冬には、新しいコートが欲しいです。でも、新しいスノーボードは欲しくないです。ス
キーへ行きたいです。でも、キャンプはしたくないです。

春 1. _____

　2. _____

　3. _____

　4. _____

夏 5. _____

　6. _____

　7. _____

　8. _____

秋 9. _____

　10. _____

　11. _____

　12. _____

冬 13. _____

　14. _____

　15. _____

　16. _____

四 For each of the seasonal items that you want above, write here something that must be done (〜しなければなりません) before you can have them.

例：冬には、新しいコートが欲しいです。お金を持って、デパートへ行って、買わなければなりません。

1.（春）_____

2.（夏）_____

3.（秋）_____

4.（冬）_____

五 Jun and his Australian friend Bruce are discussing what they would want to have or take if they were stranded on top of Mt. Everest. Rewrite each phrase in Japanese, using the cue if one is provided. Use the example as a model.

例：Jun: What sort of clothes would you want?（どんな、〜欲しい）
<u>エベレストの上には、どんな服が欲しいですか。</u>

Bruce: warm ones (*adj* + の)
<u>そうね。暖かいのが欲しいでしょう。</u>

Jun: What sort of food would you want?

1. _____

Bruce: tasty

2. _____

Jun: What sort of vehicle would you want?（車）

3. _____

Bruce: a fast one

4. _____

Jun: What sort of movie would you take?（持って行く）

5. _____

Bruce: an interesting one

6. _____

Jun: What sort of book would you take?

7. _____

Bruce: a scary one

8. _____

Jun: What sort of drink would you want?

9. _____

Bruce: a hot one

10. _____

Jun: What sort of friend would you want?

11. _____

Bruce: (free choice answer)

12. _____

Jun: What sort of (free choice question)?

13. _____

Bruce: (free choice answer)

14. _____

六 Practice the stroke order for each *kanji* below by writing the first stroke in the first box, the first and second strokes in the next box, etc. Fill in remaining boxes with complete *kanji* and the extra rows with previously learned *kanji* you need to practice.

漫												
画												
由												
治												
代												
疲												
様												
南												
内												

名前：　　　　　　　　　　　　　　　　　　　　　　　　月　　　　日

一 Trace the stroke order in the boxes, and then fill in the rest with the *kanji*.

庭	`	亠	广	广	庐	庍	庄	庭	庭	庭		
				庭						庭		
松	一	十	才	木	朳	松	松	松				
			松				松					

二 Review: Write the following in the most appropriate combination of Japanese characters (*kanji* and *kana*).

1. Enter the park, then turn left, and cross the bridge. (〜て form)

   _____

2. That pine tree is shorter than this pine tree, isn't it? (より…もっと)

   _____

3. Can you hear that frog croaking? (ケロケロ、〜える)

   _____

4. You must read that manga. (〜なければなりません)

   _____

三 Circle the *kanji* that doesn't belong with the others and then state why.

1. 注　疲　治　洗　漫　_____
2. 横　桜　様　大　松　_____
3. 英　薬　花　茶　簡　_____
4. 朝　危　昼　夜　夕　_____
5. 鬼　女　妹　男　弟　_____
6. 庭　園　内　度　肉　_____

四 Emi and Hanako are talking about Mark, a mutual friend. Finish their conversation using the English cues, but use the plain form. Then write your own conclusion to the dialogue and answer the comprehension question.

花子：エミさん、マーク君とデートに＿＿＿＿＿＿＿＿＿＿＿＿＿＿＿＿＿＿？
have the experience of going

エミ：ううん、デート＿＿＿＿＿＿＿＿＿＿＿＿＿＿＿＿＿。
didn't have the experience of going

花子：それじゃ、マーク君に電話を＿＿＿＿＿＿＿＿＿＿＿＿＿＿＿？
it's OK to call

エミ：ううん、電話を＿＿＿＿＿＿＿＿＿＿＿＿＿＿。
please don't do it

花子：それじゃ、マーク君と一緒に＿＿＿＿＿＿＿＿＿＿＿＿＿＿？
　　　　　　　　　　　いっしょ is it OK to cook yakisoba

エミ：ううん、しないで。

花子：それじゃ、マーク君とデートしてもいい？ボーイフレンドに＿＿＿＿＿＿＿。
want to make

エミ：ううん、デートしてはだめ。マーク君をボーイフレンドにしないで。でも、
＿＿＿＿＿＿＿＿＿＿＿＿＿＿＿＿＿＿＿。
free choice

Comprehension questions:

Describe how you think Hanako and Emi each feel about Mark.

＿＿＿＿＿＿＿＿＿＿＿＿＿＿＿＿＿＿＿＿＿＿＿＿＿＿＿＿＿＿＿＿＿＿＿＿＿

＿＿＿＿＿＿＿＿＿＿＿＿＿＿＿＿＿＿＿＿＿＿＿＿＿＿＿＿＿＿＿＿＿＿＿＿＿

五 Practice the stroke order for each *kanji* below by writing the first stroke in the first box, the first and second strokes in the next box, etc. Fill in remaining boxes with complete *kanji* and the extra rows with previously learned *kanji* you need to practice.

庭												
松												
漫												
画												

由											
治											
代											

六 For each action in the "Action Circle", decide whether you want someone to do it for you (〜して欲しい), or not (〜して欲しくない). Rewrite each action, in Japanese, in the appropriate box. Below the boxes, write two complete sentences using 〜して欲しい and two complete sentences using 〜して欲しくない.

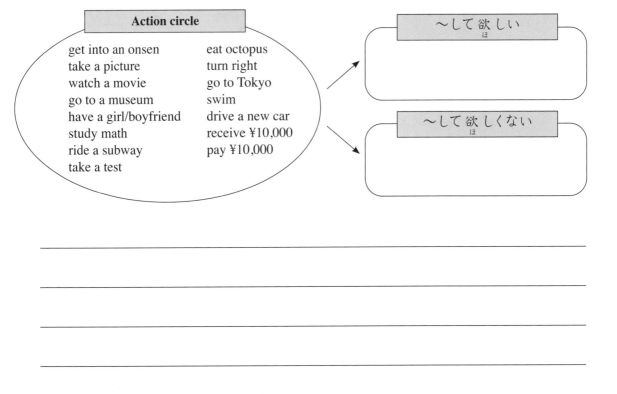

Action circle

get into an onsen
take a picture
watch a movie
go to a museum
have a girl/boyfriend
study math
ride a subway
take a test

eat octopus
turn right
go to Tokyo
swim
drive a new car
receive ¥10,000
pay ¥10,000

〜して欲しい

〜して欲しくない

INTERMEDIATE JAPANESE
アクティビティーブック

7-4

名前：　　　　　　　　　　　　　　　　　　　　月　　　日

一 Trace the stroke order in the boxes, and then fill in the rest with the *kanji*.

飯 ／ 八 今 今 今 食 食 飯 飯 飯 飯
飯　　　　　　　　飯

二 Review: Write the following in the most appropriate combination of Japanese characters (*kanji* and *kana*).

1. Wouldn't you like to eat dinner together next (week) Saturday?

   _____

2. Please read this manga freely.

   _____

3. I intend to sleep more than 12 hours. (つもり、以上)

   _____

4. If you travel to Tokyo, you must go to Ueno Park. (〜ば、〜なければなりません)

   _____

三 Mark is going with a group of Japanese friends to a place called ダンスホール『柿食えば』. It is a new dance hall in Shinagawa. He wants to be sure he understands all the rules (規則) before he goes, so he tried to translate this list into English. Help him by filling in the blanks.

ダンス・ホール柿食えばの規則

① タバコを吸ってはいけません。
② 女性はハイヒールを履いてはだめです。
③ 銃を持って来てはいけません。
④ 切符を買わなければなりません。
⑤ 一人でダンスをしてもいいです。
⑥ 18歳以上でなければなりません。
⑦ 歌わなくても良いです。
⑧ 麻薬を使ってはだめです。
⑨ アスピリンを飲んでもいいです。
⑩ 踊らなければなりません。
⑪ 柿を食べなくても良いです。

① _____ tobacco _____

② _____ shoes

③ _____ guns

④ _____ ticket

⑤ _____ dance _____

⑥ 18 years old _____

⑦ _____ sing

⑧ _____ drugs

⑨ _____ aspirin

⑩ _____ dance

⑪ _____ persimmons.

四 Unscramble the sentences below so that they match the English.

1. 20歳以上の　です　お酒を　人は　日本では　飲んでも良い

　_____

　In Japan, anyone over the age of 20 can drink liquor.

2. 規則　きびしくない　学校の　です　は
　き そく

　_____

　My school's rules are not strict.

3. ご飯　お母さんは　と言いました　時間　の　ですよ
　はん

　_____

　Your mother said, "It's time to eat!"

4. から　乗馬　欲しいです　大好き　です　が　馬　が
　　　じょうば　ほ　　　　　　　　　　　　　　うま

　_____

　I love horseback riding, so I want a horse.

5. アメリカへ　です　連れて　行って　弟は　グランド・キャニオンへ　欲しい
　　　　　　　　　　　　　　　　　　　　　　　　　　　　　　　　　ほ

　_____

　When my little brother goes to America, he wants (you) to take him to the Grand Canyon.

6. 近くの　泊まらなければ　ホテル　ハワイ　で　に　海の　なりません
   と

_____

In Hawaii, you must stay at a hotel near the ocean.

五 Practice the stroke order for each *kanji* below by writing the first stroke in the first box, the first and second strokes in the next box, etc. Fill in remaining boxes with complete *kanji* and the extra rows with previously learned *kanji* you need to practice.

飯												
以												
漫												
画												
由												
正												
朝												

名前：	月　　　日

➊ Trace the stroke order in the boxes, and then fill in the rest with the *kanji*.

願	一	厂	厂	厂	盾	盾	盾	盾	原	原	原	原
	原	願	願	願	願	願	願					
初	丶	ラ	ネ	ネ	ネ	初	初		初			
		初							初			

➋ Review: Write the following in the most appropriate combination of Japanese characters (*kanji* and *kana*).

1. Let's begin. Open your books, please.

   _____

2. Stand up. Bow. (polite phrase for "Please help me.") Sit down.

   _____

3. I would like you to come to my house (for me). (〜て欲しい)

   _____

4. Because my dog chewed (かむ) my homework, it became dirty. (から、〜くなる)

   _____

➌ You are encouraging Tetsuo, a visiting Japanese exchange student, to try some new activities and some new tastes. Rewrite the following in Japanese, and then write two of your own. Follow the example.

例：　Please try to drink this ice coffee.　→　このアイス・コーヒーを飲んでみて下さい。

1. Please try swimming in this pool.

   _____

2. My mother made this cake, so please eat some.

   _____

3. Please try to borrow this magazine.

   _____

4. Please try to go to the museum.

   _____

5. Please try to start on Page 10.

   _____

6. Please try to ride this bicycle.

   _____

7. (free choice)

   _____

8. (free choice)

   _____

四 Mark is ordering food and drink from the waitress at the ダンスホール『柿食えば』, where he went with his friends. Unfortunately, he is having a hard time understanding her. Restate her lines in English. Then fill in the blanks with the food and drink you think Mark is trying to order.

ウェイトレス： いらっしゃいませ。何名様ですか。

   _____

マーク： _____

ウェイトレス： はい、どうぞ、こちらへ。お飲み物は、何にしますか。

   _____

マーク： _____

ウェイトレス： はい、かしこまりました。りんごのジュースを一杯ですね。食べ物はいかがですか。今日、美味しいカステラがあります。食べてみませんか。

   _____

   _____

   _____

   _____

マーク： _____

ウェイトレス： はい、分かりました。ダイエット中でしたら、ケーキは食べてはいけません
ね。それでは、ご飯と味噌汁はいかがですか。
　　　　　　　　　　　はん　　み　そ しる

_____

_____

マーク： _____

ウェイトレス： はい、分かりました。パンもご飯も食べてはいけないんですね。それで
は、フルーツはいかがですか。今日は美味しい柿がありますよ。食べてみ
ませんか。　　　　　　　　　　はん　　　　　　　　　　　かき

_____

_____

マーク： _____

ウェイトレス： はい、分かりました。少々お待ち下さい。
　　　　　　　　　　　　　しょうしょう

_____

五 Practice the stroke order for each *kanji* below by writing the first stroke in the first box, the first and second strokes in the next box, etc. Fill in remaining boxes with complete *kanji* and the extra rows with previously learned *kanji* you need to practice.

願												
初												
飯												
以												
庭												
松												
漫												

												画
												由
												治
												代
												疲
												知
												動
												北
												出
												遠
												近

六 Read the haiku below then rewrite it in English.

柿くえば　　　　　_____

鐘が鳴るなり　　_____

法隆寺　　　　　_____

　　　　　（正岡子規）

* 柿: persimmon; くう: to eat; 鐘: bell; 鳴る: to ring, to sound; 法隆寺: Houryuuji temple

七 The following essay was written without much *kanji* and has been partially edited. Write *kanji* over the underlined hiragana, remembering to also write any necessary okurigana to finish words. Then, answer the comprehension questions below.

康祐君は<u>わたし</u>の*<u>いとこ</u>(cousin)で、アメリカ<u>じん</u>です。<u>じゅうごさい</u>で、まだ<u>こども</u>です。でも、<u>ちいさい</u>ときからずっと<u>いまも</u><u>じどうしゃ</u>が<u>だいすき</u>です。<u>まいにち</u><u>くるま</u>に<u>のりた</u><u>くて</u>、<u>くるま</u>の 運 転 を<u>したがっていました</u>。<u>せんしゅう</u>の<u>にちようび</u>に、おばさんは、「はい、ちょっとだけ 運 転 <u>してもいい</u>ですよ」と<u>いって</u>、康祐君を<u>くるま</u>に<u>のせました</u>。うちから<u>えき</u>までは<u>ちかくて</u>、<u>とおくない</u>です。でも、康祐君は 運 転 を<u>はじめて</u>したので、ブレーキと、アクセルの 違 いがあまり<u>わかりませんでした</u>。うちから<u>えき</u>までスピードを<u>だして</u>、<u>みぎ</u> 側 にあった<u>くるま</u>になんだいも*<u>ぶつかりました</u>。<u>えき</u>に<u>ついて</u>から、おばさんは、「すぐこの<u>くるまから</u><u>おりなさい</u>。<u>いえ</u>まで<u>あるいて</u> <u>かえりなさい</u>。この<u>くるま</u>を 運 転 <u>してはいけません</u>。」と<u>いって</u>、*<u>怒</u> りました。康祐君の<u>じゅうろくさい</u>の 誕 生 <u>び</u>は<u>らいしゅう</u>ですが、まだまだ 運 転 は<u>できません</u>。康祐君はかわいそうですね。

* いとこ - cousin
　 ぶつかる - to hit
　 怒 る - to become angry

Comprehension questions:

1. What did Kosuke really want to do? _____

2. What did Kosuke's mother allow him to do? _____

3. How did that experience go? _____

7-5   INTERMEDIATE JAPANESE WORKBOOK 121

| 名前： | | 月　　　日 |

● Trace the stroke order in the boxes, and then fill in the rest with the *kanji*.

関	｜	｢	｢	｢	｢	門	門	門	門	門	門	関
---	関	関		関						関		
開	｜	｢	｢	｢	｢	門	門	門	門	門	開	開
		開					開					
閉	｜	｢	｢	｢	｢	門	門	門	門	閉	閉	
		閉					閉					
台	ㄥ	ㄙ	台	台	台							
		台						台				
始	ㄑ	女	女	妁	妁	妁	始	始				
		始						始				
次	丶	冫	冫	冫	次	次		次				
		次					次					
集	ノ	イ	イ	亻	什	作	作	隹	隹	隼	集	集
		集						集				
伝	ノ	イ	イ	仁	伝	伝		伝				
		伝					伝					

二 Review: Write the following in the most appropriate combination of Japanese characters (*kanji* and *kana*).

1. Please try to open that door. (〜てみる)

   _____

2. Let's close that window at 11 p.m.

   _____

3. I cannot read for more than five hours. (以上、〜事が出来る)

   _____

4. Is math your next class? Well then, let's walk from here to that classroom over there. (それでは)

   _____

三 Match the appropriate Japanese phrase to each situation.

1. _____ the window is open but it's starting to rain
2. _____ the class has already begun
3. _____ the door is already halfway shut
4. _____ your group of friends has already gathered
5. _____ you are up late, and tell your mother you're worried about oversleeping
6. _____ you collect your school books together to put in your backpack
7. _____ you can hear the cricket chirping outside
8. _____ your teacher asks you to take out your homework

(ア) 開けます　　　　(キ) 聞く　　　　　　(ス) 集まっています
(イ) 開いています　　(ク) 聞こえる　　　　(セ) 集めて
(ウ) 始まっていました　(ケ) 閉めて　　　　　(ソ) 起こして
(エ) 始めて　　　　　(コ) 閉まっています　　(タ) 起きる
(オ) 見る　　　　　　(サ) 出して
(カ) 見える　　　　　(シ) 出て

四 Restate each of the following in English.

A-さん： 東京から京都まで新幹線で二時間十五分かかります。(かかる – takes [time])

   _____

B-さん： 速いですね。グリーン車の切符をおばさんから貰いましたか。

   _____

A-さん： ええ、貰いました。午前十時のグリーン車の指定席ですから、早く行かなくてもいいでしょう。

   _____

B-さん：　いえいえ！だめですよ。もう9時半です。駅で皆と集まるので、今から行かなけれ
　　　　ばなりません。それに、新幹線のドアは時間通りに閉まりますよ。遅れてはい
　　　　けません。さあ、走りましょう。

五 Practice the stroke order for each *kanji* below by writing the first stroke in the first box, the first and second strokes in the next box, etc. Fill in remaining boxes with complete *kanji* and the extra rows with previously learned *kanji* you need to practice.

関											
開											
閉											
台											
始											
次											
集											
伝											
疲											
配											
様											

名前： | 月　　　日

● Trace the stroke order in the boxes, and then fill in the rest with the *kanji*.

考	一	十	土	耂	耂	考		考			
				考						考	

● Review: Write the following in the most appropriate combination of Japanese characters (*kanji* and *kana*).

1. I cannot become more sad than this. (以上、〜くなる)

   _____

2. Her mother said, "I would like you to help me (around the house)." (〜てほしい)

   _____

3. If you finish your homework early, won't you come to my house? (〜たら、〜ませんか)

   _____

4. It rained, then I went for a walk, and then I got (became) wet. (びしょびしょ)

   _____

● You have just arrived at your homestay and are showing your host brother Sadayoshi a family photo from a recent holiday meal. He is making comments about each family member. Respond to each of his statements.

1. 妹さんは背が高そうだ。_____

2. おじいさんは元気そうだ。_____

3. 弟さんは頭が良さそうだ。_____

4. お母さんは優しそうだ。_____

5. 美味しい食べ物が食べられそうだ。_____

6. お父さんは忙しそうだ。_____

7. アメリカのサンクスギビングは楽しそうだ。_____

④ Write down an action that MUST precede each of these activities. Use 〜なければなりません.

例： go to the restaurant　→　レストランへ行く前に、バスに乗らなければなりません。

eat dinner　_____

write a folk tale　_____

smoke tobacco　_____

study haiku　_____

try (to eat) natto　_____

draw a picture　_____

ride on a boat　_____

take a bath　_____

⑤ Practice the stroke order for each *kanji* below by writing the first stroke in the first box, the first and second strokes in the next box, etc. Fill in remaining boxes with complete *kanji* and the extra rows with previously learned *kanji* you need to practice.

考													
関													
開													
閉													
台													
始													
知													

名前： | 月　　　日

● Review: Write the following in the most appropriate combination of Japanese characters (*kanji* and *kana*).

1. Please try to close that window. (〜てみる)

_____

2. I was thinking about the earthquake.

_____

3. The only thing he has done is to study Russian. (だけ、〜した事がある)

_____

4. That bridge seems scary. (〜そうだ)

_____

● Fill in the blanks below with an appropriate phrase.

例： 桜が＊咲いている時に<u>外で散歩するのが大好きです</u>。
　　　When the cherry trees bloom, I love to walk outside.

1. 小さい時に、_____

2. _____ 時に、お腹が痛くなる。

3. 飛行機に乗る時に、_____

4. _____ 時に、よく勉強しました。

5. 忙しい時に、_____

6. _____ 時に、ドアと窓を開けておきます。

＊咲く - to bloom

● Practice the stroke order for each *kanji* below by writing the first stroke in the first box, the first and second strokes in the next box, etc. Fill in remaining boxes with complete *kanji* and the extra rows with previously learned *kanji* you need to practice.

考												
浜												
止												
忙												
寒												
遠												
怖												

④ Kanji Review: Use the space below to write as many adjectives containing *kanji* that you have learned as you can. Try to keep opposite pairs together.

名前：　　　　　　　　　　　　　　　　　　　　　月　　　　　日

⚊ Trace the stroke order in the boxes, and then fill in the rest with the *kanji*.

困	丨	冂	円	闬	闲	困	困			
			困				困			

⚋ Review: Write the following in the most appropriate combination of Japanese characters (*kanji* and *kana*).

1. Try to move that heavy rock. (〜てみる)

   _____

2. Be sure to bring a gift with you. (きっと)

   _____

3. When I eat cake, I cannot stop. (〜事が出来ません)

   _____

4. That kite (たこ) appears very light (in weight). Please show it to me. (〜そうだ)

   _____

⚌ Pair each simple statement with the closest expanded sentence below by writing the number next to the letter on the blank. Then write your own version of an expanded sentence on the blanks on the following page.

simple sentence
1. 橋を渡っています。
2. これは本です。
3. あのやねは重そうです。
4. 地震がありました。
5. 学校へ行きませんでした。
6. 犬がいます。

expanded sentence
_____ (A) ワンワン鳴いている犬はあの大きい石の上にいます。
_____ (B) その面白い本を絶対に読んで下さい。(絶対 = absolutely)
_____ (C) 高い建物の右がわにある橋を渡っています。
_____ (D) 近くの三階建ての喫茶店のやねは本当に重そうですね。
_____ (E) 地震のあと、お水がなくて、非常に困りました。
_____ (F) 先週、おなかも のどもとても痛くて、なかなか学校へも行けませんでした。

1. _____

2. _____

3. _____

4. _____

5. _____

6. _____

四 As you read the following story, place close attention to the underlined sections. Once you have read the entire story, look at the translation that follows. Go back to the beginning and change the underlined word forms and cut periods/add commas to make compound sentences paralleling the English paragraph below. Here are a few patterns you might use to rewrite the underlined sections:

〜時に	〜たり〜たり	〜ば
〜て form	〜が、…	〜から

毎週日曜日、おばあさんに会いに<u>行く</u>。かならず贈り物を持って行く。おばあさんが家に<u>いる</u>。よく<u>話す</u>。写真を<u>見る</u>。お茶を<u>飲む</u>。でも、時々おばあさんが家に<u>いない</u>。そうしたら、おじいさんとだけトランプを<u>する</u>。ケーキを<u>食べる</u>。

おじいさんとおばあさんは東京の飯田橋の近くに<u>住んでいる</u>。伝統的な所がたくさん<u>残っている</u>。おばあさんは日本舞踊が大好き<u>だ</u>。小さいころから今までずっと踊りを<u>している</u>。毎週二回か三回、踊りの教室へ<u>行く</u>。おじいさんは、前に　踊って　いた。今はもう踊らない。一年前に、舞踊教室で、*<u>倒れた</u>。足を*折ってしまった。おじいさんに<u>聞いてみる</u>。「踊りは危ないよ。」とよく言う。

* 倒れる - to collapse, to fall over
* 折ってしまった – to break, to fracture

Translation:

Every Monday, when we go to meet grandmother, we take presents with us. When we are at grandmother's, we talk a lot. We do things like look at photos, and drink tea. But sometimes she's not there. Then, with grandfather, we do things like play cards and eat cake.

Grandfather and grandmother live near Tokyo's Iidabashi. There are a lot of traditional places left there. Grandmother loves Japanese dance, dancing it since she was young. Two or three times every week she goes to dance class. Grandfather used to dance too, but he doesn't dance anymore. One year ago, at dance class, he fell and broke his leg. Now, if you ask grandfather, he often says, "Dancing is dangerous!"

Practice the stroke order for each *kanji* below by writing the first stroke in the first box, the first and second strokes in the next box, etc. Fill in remaining boxes with complete *kanji* and the extra row with a previously learned *kanji* you need to practice.

重												
困												
考												
関												
開												
閉												
台												
始												
次												
集												
伝												
疲												
知												
配												
怖												

名前：　　　　　　　　　　　　　　　　　　　　　　月　　　日

⚊ Trace the stroke order in the boxes, and then fill in the rest with the *kanji*.

走	一	十	土	キ	キ	走	走				
			走						走		

⚋ Review: Write the following in the most appropriate combination of Japanese characters (*kanji* and *kana*).

1. At Disneyland, you can do things like meet Mickey Mouse and ride scary roller coasters. (〜たり 〜たり)

   _____

2. Once you receive this, you must go (out) quickly. (〜ば、〜しなければなりません)

   _____

3. I would like you to observe (まもる) these rules. (〜して欲しい)

   _____

4. Because the weather is extremely hot, I want watermelon. (〜が欲しい)

   _____

⚌ Use the Verb Appendix to help you with this exercise. First, think of a dangerous situation. Then, think of an action you should or should not do in that situation. Write your warning here. Use the example below as a model.

例：バスに乗ったら、立たないで下さい。

1. _____

2. _____

3. _____

4. _____

5. _____

6. _____

7. _____

8. _____

四 You are well known for giving good advice. Some of your Japanese friends have gone and done some things they regret, and now they are asking you for advice. Their problems are in Column A. Write your suggestions in Column B. The first one is done for you.

Column A	Column B
母の誕生日のプレゼントのお金を全部 たんじょうび 使ってしまいました。	お母さんに手作りのスカーフと手作りのケーキをあげて下さい。
ボーイフレンドに「さようなら」と言ってしまいました。	
化学の教科書をなくしてしまいました。 か　　　きょうかしょ	
友達に喫茶店に　行こうと言ったのに、 きっさ もうお金を全部使ってしまいました。	
弟のズボンをはいてしまいました。	
旅館で違う部屋に入ってしまいました。 りょ　　ちが　　へや	
ルームメートの帽子がなくなってしまいました。 ぼうし	

五 Practice the stroke order for each *kanji* below by writing the first stroke in the first box, the first and second strokes in the next box, etc. Fill in remaining boxes with complete *kanji* and the extra rows with previously learned *kanji* you need to practice.

走												

重
困
考
飯
暑
松
庭
漫
画
由
疲
危
暖

名前：　　　　　　　　　　　　　　　　　　　　　　| 月　　　日

一 Trace the stroke order in the boxes, and then fill in the rest with the *kanji*.

覚	丶	丷	丷	丷	丷	当	尚	尚	尚	覚	覚
			覚						覚		
式	一	二	丅	工	式	式		式			
		式							式		
急	丿	勹	夕	刍	刍	刍	急	急	急		急
		急							急		

二 Review: Write the following in the most appropriate combination of Japanese characters (*kanji* and *kana*).

1. Please memorize (learn) the *kanji* for "peace." (覚える)

   _____

2. Yesterday, I went and completely ran a marathon. (〜てしまう)

   _____

3. Hurry up! I'm in trouble! (急ぐ、困る)

   _____

4. When I was in middle school 2nd year, we had a wonderful beginning-of-the-school-year ceremony. (〜の時に、入学式)

   _____

三 Practice the stroke order for each *kanji* below by writing the first stroke in the first box, the first and second strokes in the next box, etc. Fill in remaining boxes with complete *kanji* and the extra rows with previously learned *kanji* you need to practice.

覚											

式														
急														
走														
重														
困														
止														

四 Connect each event with the time it occurred.

Time	Event
四月	北海道でたいてい雪が降り始める
1868年	キリスト教の信者が教会へ行く
105年AD	桜と入学式
十二月	忘年会がよくある
日曜日	アメリカのノースカロライナで、ライト兄弟が最初の飛行機を飛ばす
1900年	明治維新があった
十一月	中国で紙を発明した

五 地図 Directions: You have traveled through much of Japan with our characters. However, you've not visited the island of Shikoku. You and a Japanese friend will go there this summer, but your friend knows nothing about Shikoku and wants information about what to see and do while there. Draw a map of Shikoku (including part of the southern coast of Honshu) in the box below. Below your map, write a draft of an email to your friend. You may write about:

- varieties of ways to get between the two islands
- 5-6 places to go sightseeing
- two or three different types of accommodations
- specialty foods to sample
- local goods or handicrafts that might make good souvenirs

Your email should be between 300 and 400 characters in length and your writing should be done within 20 minutes of starting. Typing your email is optional.

_____

_____

_____

_____

_____

_____

_____

_____

_____

_____

_____

_____

名前：　　　　　　　　　　　　　　　　　　　　　| 月　　　　日

● Interview a Japanese person or an acquaintance who is quite knowledgeable about Japan. Also interview two other people who know this person. Ask a variety of questions about what the interviewees' interests and special knowledge about Japan. Plan your interview by writing a list of questions, then record notes from each of your interviews.

Pre-interview question brainstorming

1. _____

2. _____

3. _____

4. _____

5. _____

6. _____

7. _____

8. _____

9. _____

10. _____

Notes from interview 1:

_____

_____

_____

_____

_____

_____

_____

_____

_____

_____

_____

Notes from interview 2:

_____

_____

_____

_____

_____

_____

_____

_____

_____

Notes from interview 3:

_____

_____

_____

_____

_____

_____

_____

_____

_____

_____

⊜ 作文: Here is your chance to consolidate the data from your interviews. In this 作文, summarize the information from your interviews. Use the patterns ～と言いました; ～と思います; ～と聞きました. Challenge yourself to vary your writing style by including at least one pattern from each chapter in this book. Remember to try to enrich your sentences with adverbs and adjectives.

_____

_____

_____

_____

_____

_____

_____

_____

_____

_____

_____

_____

_____

名前：　　　　　　　　　　　　　　　　　　　　　月　　　　日

● やり方: In the space below, write positive statements about people you know. Mention how good they are at doing what they do. Make at least 10 statements. Then elaborate on each statement.

例: 母の焼きそばの作り方はとても面白いです。人参となすも入れます。
にんじん
= My mother's method of making yakisoba is very interesting. She puts in carrots and eggplant.

1. _____
_____

2. _____
_____

3. _____
_____

4. _____
_____

5. _____
_____

6. _____
_____

7. _____
_____

8. _____
_____

9. _____
_____

10. _____
_____

⊟ Adjective word search: Find as many adjectives as you can in the grid below. The adjectives are in a variety of conjugations. Find at least 20 and write each of them in the present positive form on the lines below the grid.

わ	る	く	あ	り	ま	せ	ん	た	ん	か	っ	ま	す	か	せ	あ	た
か	ま	た	ず	し	っ	い	む	あ	ま	い	く	あ	り	ま	あ	ん	な
か	く	っ	き	び	す	い	わ	た	お	そ	い	た	つ	ざ	く	ふ	し
っ	な	か	の	な	ぐ	ま	え	た	は	が	す	め	い	わ	く	こ	け
た	べ	し	な	ひ	に	ぎ	や	か	と	し	た	る	ん	だ	ね	う	し
え	っ	ろ	い	ぷ	と	し	く	く	は	か	ち	か	お	ど	す	る	こ
と	が	よ	す	き	ま	だ	ね	な	そ	っ	れ	っ	で	は	く	か	こ
れ	の	お	し	は	ず	か	し	い	り	た	お	た	た	べ	る	さ	わ
の	が	だ	い	す	し	ら	き	で	す	ね	か	れ	は	ぼ	び	く	い
の	へ	お	し	り	い	い	ぱ	っ	す	も	お	そ	ろ	し	く	な	い
で	ん	と	う	て	き	か	ん	だ	の	ほ	う	が	い	だ	す	て	ま

_____

_____

_____

_____

_____

_____

_____

_____

_____

_____

_____

_____

名前：　　　　　　　　　　　　　　　　　　　　　　　月　　　日

Letter writing: In the メール for this section in the textbook, Ben receives a message from Mr. Matsumoto. The message is about travelling from Hiroshima to Miyajima. Use your media center or the Internet to find information about 錦帯橋. Write to Ben, giving him recommendations about travelling to this site. Tell him what it is, when it was built, and any other interesting bits of information. Include instructions on how to get there from either Miyajima or Hiroshima. Use the genkoyoshi below. Begin your letter in the upper right corner, writing vertically, and skipping the first two spaces for your greeting. Indent one space for each paragraph after that. Indent two spaces for your closing. Refer to **TimeForJapanese.com** for more information. Your letter should be between 300 and 400 characters.

名前：　　　　　　　　　　　　　　　　　　　　　　　　月　　　日

Your Japanese friend needs help brainstorming answers on how to best do certain activities. Choose ten of the activities below. Then, supply suggestions for best carrying out each scenario. Use the "の為に" pattern and elaborate.

例：getting good grades: いい成績を取るために、たくさん勉強しなければなりません。

A) getting up early
B) studying kanji
C) working at a part-time job (アルバイト)
D) going to the mall
E) using a cell phone (携帯)
F) using an eraser
G) driving a car
H) taking an airplane

I) helping your mother
J) reading
K) cooking
L) riding a bicycle
M) riding a bus
N) using a computer
O) wearing a suit/dress

1. _____
   _____

2. _____
   _____

3. _____
   _____

4. _____
   _____

5. _____
   _____

6. _____
   _____

7. _____
   _____

8. _____
   _____

9. _____
   _____

10. _____
    _____

名前： | 月　　　　日

⚫ 自分の将来：Planning guide
　　　しょうらい

Try to look up the following in Japanese before going to English version sites. Research five post-secondary schools (colleges/universities), some near you, that offer Japanese courses. Include: school name, contact address/email/phone, level of possible achievement (language courses only, minor/major, Japanese literature courses, etc.)

1. _____

_____

2. _____

_____

3. _____

_____

4. _____

_____

5. _____

_____

⚫ Do any of the above schools offer exchange opportunities in Japan? If so, which ones and what are the options?

_____

_____

_____

_____

_____

_____

_____

_____

_____

三 地図: Research two post-secondary schools in the Kansai area, two schools in the Kanto area, and two schools in another area of Japan that offer exchange opportunities. Then, draw a map of Japan below showing the locations of these schools and other places you would like to visit.

四 Use the *kanji* list in the textbook appendix to find *kanji* containing these radicals. Find at least three *kanji* for each radical, and write them in the appropriate boxes.

日	亻	女
土	宀	水 (氵)
儿	匕	口 (くち)
厶	丶	冂, 匚, 囗

名前：　　　　　　　　　　　　　　　　　月　　　日

一 Trace the stroke order in the boxes, and then fill in the rest with the *kanji*.

牛	ノ	㇉	二	牛					牛			
匹	一	丁	兀	匹					匹			
馬	｜	厂	厂	斤	垂	馬	馬	馬	馬	馬		
鳥	｀	亻	宀	户	自	皀	鳥	鳥	鳥	鳥	鳥	
虎	｜	㇉	占	广	户	卢	庐	虎				

二 自分の 将来(しょうらい): Jobs where Japanese is spoken. Use the Internet and local resources to discover jobs in your region where Japanese language skills are either a benefit or a preferred/required condition for employment. List several of those positions below in Japanese with notes as necessary. Be prepared to discuss them.

三 What possibilities can you think of for using your Japanese language skills in the future? Describe at least three possibilities here and be prepared to discuss them in Japanese.

_____

_____

_____

_____

_____

_____

_____

_____

_____

_____

_____

_____

四 You will be participating in a debate in Japanese. Read the question below and decide which side to support. Then, organize your thoughts so as to make your argument stronger. Use the space below to plan your strategy and make some preliminary arguments.

自分の国の大学で勉強をするのと、日本の大学で勉強をするのと、どちらの方がいいですか。

1. _____

2. _____

3. _____

4. _____

5. _____

6. _____

7. _____

8. _____

9. _____

10. _____

五 Practice the stroke order for each *kanji* below by writing the first stroke in the first box, the first and second strokes in the next box, etc. Fill in remaining boxes with complete *kanji* and the extra rows with previously learned *kanji* you need to practice.

牛												
匹												
馬												
鳥												
虎												

六 Kanji Review: In the space below, write as many single *kanji* words and their meanings as you can.

例: 犬 = dog

名前：　　　　　　　　　　　　　　　　　　| 月　　　日

⊖ Pre-writing activity for テクノ時間: Use the lines below to plan your writing.

1. State your thesis or topic here:

   _____

   _____

   _____

2. Brainstorm ideas and points that expand your thesis.

3. Write an outline of at least three major points and supporting details.

   _____

   _____

   _____

   _____

   _____

   _____

   _____

   _____

   _____

   _____

   _____

   _____

   _____

4. Write a list of vocabulary words and *kanji* you might need for your 作文.
<small>さくぶん</small>

_____

_____

_____

_____

_____

_____

_____

_____

二 Complete the Sudoku below using the animal *kanji*.

豚			虎				羊	
								鳥
	犬	虎			牛	蛇		
	羊			豚				馬
猫			鳥				虎	
		犬				猫		
鳥								
	馬				羊			蛇
		牛	猫			犬	豚	

三 四コマ漫画 are four-panel manga that contain a story line and usually end with a twist. Use the four-panel template below to create and draw your own manga. Each panel should include dialogue (use speech bubbles). Go to **TimeForJapanese.com** for examples.

名前： | 月   日

将来 (しょうらい)：Your friend 友弘 (ひろ) in Japan is curious about the sort of occupational possibilities that are available for students in your school. Talk to your closest friends about their plans for a future career. Consider your own hopes as well, then write an email to 友弘 on this topic. Organize your thoughts in paragraph form (not basic sentences). Remember to have an introduction, a middle, and a summary to your writing. Use the genkoyoshi below, starting your letter in the upper right corner skipping the first two spaces for your greeting, then indenting one space for each paragraph after that. Indent two spaces for your closing. Be sure to write vertically. Your letter should be between 300 and 400 characters in length.

名前：　　　　　　　　　　　　　　　　　　　　　　　月　　　　日

① Draw lines to match each Japanese proverb with its closest English equivalent.

石の上にも三年   Like father, like son

花より団子
　　だん ご   Perseverance overcomes all

蛙 の子は 蛙
かえる　　　　 かえる   Pearls before swine

ばかにつける薬はない   Even monkeys fall from trees

さるも木から落ちる
　　　　　　　お   Dumplings before flowers

猫に 小判
　　 こ ばん   No cure for a fool

② As far as we know, 友 continues his travels. Or perhaps he has returned to his family in 四国. In the space below, write the next chapter in Tomo's adventures. Include an introduction, a middle, and a conclusion to your writing. Do your best to use complex sentences and transitional words. Expand your sentences by using elaborative details such as times, places, adjectives and adverbs.

_____

_____

_____

_____

_____

_____

_____

_____

_____

_____